THE BAREFOOT ACCOUNTANT

The BAREFOOT ACCOUNTANT

by

Jonathon Clark

ILLUSTRATIONS BY MARK RICHARDS

BREWIN BOOKS

First published August 1990
by Brewin Books, Studley, Warwickshire. B80 7LG

ISBN 0 947731 72 5

Typeset in Baskerville 11pt.
and made and printed in Great Britain
by Supaprint (Redditch)Ltd.,
Redditch, Worcestershire.

Dedicated to the Angels of Transformation and Purpose
who guided this work and to my father, bless him, who
would give away his last penny.

CONTENTS

INTRODUCTION

Life as Financial Director of an engineering company used to be so straightforward.

Looking back at the advanced age of thirty-two, there was the knowledge that success had already been achieved through a series of examination passes and rapid promotions, while stretching down the years to retirement the obvious goal was to become Managing Director with the accompanying Daimler, Share Options and Executive Bonus Scheme, paid directly from Head Office.

Life became a little less simple once he realised that plants could talk.

The use of meditation in management meetings was something with which the business world of Walsall was largely unfamiliar in the mid-nineteen-eighties - almost as unfamiliar as the various spiritual communities which he visited were with the benefits of financial management.

THE BAREFOOT ACCOUNTANT by Jonathon Clark is an account of his attempts to bridge these apparently separate worlds. These attempts have not always been successful but they all add to an understanding of life - or so he keeps telling himself!

CHAPTER 1

THE BAREFOOT ACCOUNTANT

For much of the period from September 1986 until November 1988 I felt as though I were the inhabitant of two different worlds.

On the one hand I would dress in a suit and tie each morning, carry my briefcase to the fuel-injected company car and drive up the motorway whilst listening to cassettes on the stereo system; after an average journey time of twenty-six minutes and eighteen seconds as calculated by the on-board computer I would arrive at a factory where I occupied the post of Finance Director.

The company employed six hundred people and their work was to change the shape of different metals by various processes; I was responsible for all the usual things for which a Finance Director is responsible and which can be found in any specification for such a job. These include such items as "monthly and statutory accounts," "annual budgets," "control of cash flow," "the establishment and maintenance of financial systems of information," "returns to Companies House" and "full participation at Board Level in the Commercial Decisions of the Company."

We carefully budgeted and recorded our profits, delayed payments to our suppliers whilst expecting our debtors to clear their accounts with us promptly and observed such rituals of enforced jollity as the Christmas Dinner at which Directors, Staff and their respective partners mingled a trifle uneasily; the Workers, for the most part, boycotted such events due to a collective suspicion borne from years of adversarial industrial relations.

I received Memos from Head Office such as:

"It is procedure for Directors of subsidiary companies to have their expenses approved by their Managing Director and for those of the Managing Director to be approved by his appropriate [Parent Company] link Director. Would any persons not complying with this procedure instigate arrangements immediately and be aware auditors are likely to pay particular attention to these systems in future."

In September of 1986 I visited the Findhorn Foundation in North-East Scotland (a community "into market

1

gardening and meditation" as a recent newspaper article put it, rather superficially) and, like Alice in Wonderland, I stepped through the door into my own sub-conscious, into a world where decisions were made by consensus - democracy being considered a failed option, never mind the authoritarian approach of most parts of British Industry. It was a world where people talked to plants - more importantly it was a world where plants talked to people - and where throwing one's arms around one's fellow worker was the norm rather than an action which was likely to lead to a dismissal for sexual harassment.

It was a world of make believe - or so it seemed to someone like myself with the rigorous training of an accountant; people talked about writing cheques with love and paying for things when they were needed regardless of the bank balance in the knowledge that the money would appear at the right time - something called the Laws of Manifestation.

From Findhorn I was led to a further exploration of this other world - a world unfamiliar and yet half remembered like the magical tune which is heard in the distance one summer's evening but cannot be totally recalled the next morning.

I read things like:

"Ideally in the New Age, 'No management is good management,' because we should all be co-creating through universal attunement to the will of God."

Opposite that quotation was a cartoon showing a computer spewing out a Financial Report; the lady is reading from the report and says to the man standing next to her, "It says 'be still, turn within, know that all is very very well," - the words which Eileen Caddy, one of the founders of Findhorn, heard from her Inner Voice. I wondered what my Managing Director would say if the computer we had just purchased produced such a report.

In both environments I began to feel as though I were a fish out of water. Inevitably, my enthusiasm for the World of Spirit spilled over into my everyday work but there were few people in the Industrial Heartlands of the West Midlands with whom to share this; except for a few close friends I was either greeted with disbelief or marked down for an early bus to the loony bin.

Despite this growing sense of alienation in the Business World I could not totally reject my long training and years of experience in it and I would often grow impatient at the mess in which my new found friends landed themselves and which could have easily been avoided by using good old management techniques.

It took me two years before I bowed to the inevitable and released the ambitions I had held in my twenties of Executive Stardom. I not only needed greater variety in my life than going to the same office nineteen days out of twenty but I knew that somehow I had to integrate these two worlds which I inhabited; more than this I began to see that these two outer worlds represented different parts of my own Being and that helping to bring these outer worlds together was a process by which I could heal and unite the fragments of my own psyche.

During the time since that first visit to Findhorn the issue of money has gained in importance for me. Now, coming from a Chartered Accountant that might sound pretty dumb as you may think it would have long been a major concern of mine.

Indeed it had, but in a rather abstract sense. Like many accountants in a senior position I found no difficulty in signing a cheque for £200,000 but the prospect of performing a spot check on the balance in the petty cash float by counting notes and coins was likely to send me into a blind panic; neither was I the best person to be Treasurer of a charity although I occupied that position on a number of occasions.

No, money started to take on a new significance as I began to realise that the way we behave with money is an accurate reflection of the way we shape much of our lives. As this realisation grew I began to have more and more "money experiences" which seemed to bear out my new understanding. Not all of these experiences were pleasant but they seemed to give credence to the theory that we draw certain experiences to ourselves in order to learn particular lessons.

What also seemed to be true was a little phrase which cropped up more and more for me in different ways such as "Imagination Creates Reality" or "As a Man Thinks So Is He" or "We Create Our Own Reality by Our Thoughts" or "Visualise Something Strongly Enough and It Will Happen." The trouble with knowing this, as my friend Andrew remarked last week, is that you have to be careful what you pray for!

As part of the integration process of the two worlds which I inhabited I finally left the Corporate Scene on 31 October 1988 in order to work as a freelance financial consultant.   My work consists of running seminars to help managers or the self employed understand the basics of a profit and loss account and balance sheet.   I also do some consultancy for a local College and I advise on insurances, pensions, mortgages and investments.   In all of this work the underlying aim is to create a safe space in which people can deal with money issues.   My range of clients is wide and encompasses everyone from the "very straight" to the "out and out New Ager."

A few weeks ago it became clear that a further way in which to expand this work of creating a safe space in which to handle money would be to write a book and my title was provisionally "For Those Who Doubt" until the final title was suggested unwittingly by my friend Carol.

We were attending a seminar and the presenter, Andrew again, observed that things were not always what they seemed these days; the range of dress, he noted, in the room encompassed one man wearing a jacket and trousers, a lady in a business suit and myself clad in a shortsleeved shirt, shorts and nothing on my feet in order to cope with the London Heat of June 1989.   I was immediately re-named the Barefoot Accountant and knew that, now I had a title with which I was happy, the book would have to be written very soon.

But, we were just about to move house which would take all my energy over the next couple of weeks. Then, in the first week of July I had three days training and two days consultancy with four different clients.

For the first time in eight months I had five days consecutive work and I didn't want it! Not only that, but in the three weeks which followed I could see the consultancy work leaving only four or five days in which to write. Then there was August and I was due to go away. . .

As a token gesture I cancelled a day's consultancy and that seemed to be a clear enough message for some mysterious unseen force to realise what I wanted.

A two day seminar was cancelled because notice of it had been circulated too late and there were not enough participants; a one day course had to be put back several weeks because of a rail strike and the consulting project which threatened to take up seven or eight days in July was re-specified and is capable of being completed in four days. The first week of July, previously booked solid, now only has one half day booked and I am free to write!

Even this process throws up a money issue. In my traditional mode of ensuring that there is sufficient work to cover bills, provide for the future and satisfy my pleasures I was having kittens at the thought of five days work at good rates disappearing into the ground. And yet, in my heart, I knew that I had created that whole situation for myself and that what was important was to write this book. My knowledge is that by doing this - by following my heart - my material needs will be met and a further part of my purpose will have been completed.

This last few days I have moved house, thrown out yet more old papers and arranged a spare bedroom into an office. The last box of rubbish went downstairs late last night and I felt as though I had been following the sort of nesting instinct that many women seem to experience in the late stages of pregnancy. As I came in from dumping the last box of rubbish I glanced at my astrological calendar and noticed that the New Moon was at 5 a.m. this morning - the perfect time for starting a project whilst the time for preparation had just passed. Unconsciously I had been clearing for three or four days, in what felt like perfect harmony with whatever universal forces are present in our lives.

This book is being written in order to share what wisdom I may have gained in the area of money and work for you, the Reader, wherever and whoever you are. I hope that you find you can laugh at some of it and that it is of help to you to know that, whilst we are alone on our journey we are also, all of us, connected.

The layout also departs from the more traditional form of continuous prose and, rather than a straight piece of narrative, I suggest you might wish to consider it more as a pool of water, some of it in light and some in shade, inviting you to experience a range of feelings as you swim in different parts at different times.

At the core there is a collection of stories about money issues, the majority of which are my personal experience although a couple of minor incidents are the stories of someone close to me. On occasion, names and places have been changed - not to "protect the innocent" but to honour the privacy of certain individuals.

Intermingled with these stories are some imagined "money situations" - many based on real-life incidents - which you may wish to try out with friends, a section on the vocabulary of money and work and a calendar of the more significant events in my own biography so that the reader may see the stories in that perspective. I have also included "The Toby Arnott Poems" which were published in the "Birmingham Post" in 1984 - the story of another accountant whose yearnings to travel barefoot were never quite realised!

CHAPTER 2

THE ROLLRIGHT STONES

The main road which runs from Stratford-on-Avon to Oxford, the A34, is one on which I have driven for the past seventeen years. I would avoid it if I could but, faced with the necessity of a car journey to London then I prefer the A34 to the perennial traffic jams on the M1 motorway.

Traffic rarely comes to a standstill on the A34, it just never moves very fast due to a mixture of sharp bends and heavily laden trucks ferrying automotive components between the car factories of Oxford and Birmingham. More recently I have come to view this road as a great assistant in my spiritual journeying for it has the facility to teach patience - a commodity which seems to have been in short supply when my hand of cards was dealt for this lifetime.

Another positive aspect of this usually slow stretch of forty miles is that I have the opportunity to view some of the loveliest countryside of England - the sort of stuff which, if it could be put into a bottle, would be sold as "Essence of England" to the tourists who throng the souvenir shops of Oxford and Stratford.

In the forty mile drive there are three major round-abouts, almost at equal distances apart, and an obvious sense, after twenty miles, that the halfway point has been reached. This feeling can be noticed on the long, gentle hill which lies just to the south of the village of Long Compton and is one of the few places where the road is straight enough to overtake other cars and lorries - many of the latter being slowed by the incline. Slowly, slowly up the hill and then there is a road sign which announces that you are leaving Warwickshire and passing into Oxfordshire.

On a July evening in 1988 I was returning from a day's work near London and, with many thoughts in my mind, was in no hurry to get back to Birmingham; I saw the journey as some space in which to think, to toss over some new ideas, to sieve the myriad of grains in my head and see if somehow I could bake a decent loaf of them.

Feeling a little tired and needing some air I resolved to stop at the halfway point on the A34 and visit the Rollright Stones.

7

These stones, about seventy in number - although legend has it that they cannot be counted accurately - have stood in a circle on the site for thousands of years; the guide books will tell you such facts more exactly and it does not seem relevant here to worry about their precise history. What I did know was that they represented a temporary refuge for me and held fond memories of the previous summer when I had enjoyed a wonderful picnic with my children and my parents.

It had been the weekend of the Harmonic Convergence, an astrological event of considerable significance. At this time eight of the ten planets were in Fire signs (Aries, Leo and Sagittarius) making what is known as a Grand Trine in Fire. That weekend also marked the end of the twenty-six thousand year cycle of the Aztec calendar and the sun shone solidly for two days as if to fill us all with new hope. For years I had ignored the Stones but now I was beginning to know that they were important, even if I did not fully understand why.

The road dipped and rose, twisted and straightened and twisted again for twenty miles north of Oxford until the sign at the side of the road announced that I would be passing into Warwickshire. I turned left and drove along the small lane between the high hedges for perhaps half a mile and parked the car.

To my surprise there was no-one else there although it was early evening in the height of summer when I would have expected visitors. I got out of the car and passed through the little copse of trees that guard the entrance to the circle. A dilapidated stone building sported a sign asking for money for the animal sanctuary and I dipped into the little bag I used to carry documents and money removing all the silver and bronze; there was not a great deal there.

I left the hut and entered the stone circle. What had these stones meant when they were first erected; were they to be used for navigational purposes, for telling the time or might there have been some more sinister reason for their existence? No, despite seeing films like "Raiders of the Lost Ark" and "Indiana Jones and the Temple of Doom" I could not believe that anything sinister had ever taken place in this beautiful part of the world, not in this green and pleasant land.

I stood in the centre of the circle, placed the bag at my feet and closed my eyes. The peace there was very beautiful, particularly after the noise and aggression of the corporate business of the day and the changes which I knew were forcing themselves painfully, inexorably and necessarily into my life.

In my pocket I had a pack of Angel Cards. These are produced by the Findhorn Foundation and are very simple, beautiful drawings of Angels representing various qualities which we might like to invoke into our lives to help us. I reached into my pocket and drew the Angel of Patience - a message, it seemed, for my whole life.

I closed my eyes again and the word "Light" came into my mind. Almost at once I connected this to a time, some twelve months earlier when I had been doing a lot of running, in itself a form of meditation. The word "light" had been with me at that time; the message seemed not so much to do with becoming enlightened but with learning to live more lightly.

As if guided by some unseen hand - I doubt whether my rational mind would have sanctioned it - I proceeded to empty out the remaining coins from my bag until none were left. I think I had no notes in my wallet that evening so this represented my last cash until I got to a bank. There were twelve £1 coins on the ground and I proceeded to arrange them in a circle, alternately head and tail on top.

I then stood up and said "I place these coins here as a symbol of my trust in the Universe," and walked out of the stone circle feeling very light and very calm.

As ever, I could see two sides to this incident. On the one hand my Chartered Accountant/Saturn/Adult/Authority half was saying something like:

"Are you crazy? You spend years training to be an accountant, learning about financial control, writing reports telling clients how to guard their money and then you just go and throw the stuff on the ground. All I can say is I hope the Institute of Chartered Accountants never gets to hear about this!"

And the other, older, intuitive, childlike part is saying "Just trust."

So I get back to Birmingham, chew the fat with some friends who are round to dinner about how we dislike our jobs and how the system is against us and our protests expose the fact that we are refusing to take any responsibility for the world which we have created and which we have decided to inhabit.

I grew up believing, because that is the way I was taught, in the separateness of academic disciplines. After all, when I was at school it was the accepted norm that boys studied Science and girls studied Arts.

Boys did woodwork and girls did cookery even though natural ability might indicate that a switch from the usual roles would be both appropriate and desirable.

Science and religion were also areas which did not appear compatible. And then there was this thing called Spirituality that seemed to be going around - was that the same as religion? Or opposed to it? Boy, did I have some sorting out to do!

So here was this idea I had picked up from some spiritual teacher somewhere that said "Whatever you put out will come back" and which was sometimes hard to see because there was no logic to it until I remembered that I had learned the same thing twenty years earlier when my Physics teacher told me about Newton's Third Law which says that to every action there is an equal and opposite reaction. It took me a long time to realise that if you walk far enough in a straight line you find it is not a straight line at all but a circle and, eventually, you reach the point where you started.

I tried to convince my Chartered Accountant/Saturn/ Adult half that this was the case and that my £12 would come back but the response was less than enthusiastic. One

11

of the important points about this Law of the Universe is to recognise that whatever you require in your life, whether it is money or anything else, will come in if you allow it and, importantly, it may well come in from an unexpected source. Don't be too attached to the origin - just give thanks for its arrival!

At that time we were part of a programme hosting a group of disabled soldiers from Israel. That in itself was a test of learning not to judge people for, much as I was reviled by the television coverage of daily acts of violence which the Israelis appeared to be perpetrating, the reality of my world was different. Staying in our house was a twenty-nine year old man who longed to be able to play football again but who could not do so because there was so much metal holding his legs together. How could I reject him?

The day after I had been to the Rollright Stones was the last day which the Israelis were spending in Birmingham and we attended a tea party for the group in the afternoon. As we walked home a passing car stopped containing two of our friends who had been at the party. We talked through the car window about possible plans for the evening; maybe we could go to a country pub to give the soldiers a last taste of Olde England or maybe they would get together for a sing-song.

"Well," said Jo through the car window, "I know what our soldier wants to do and that is to go to the Casino. The whole group went earlier in the week and he loved it but I can't take him because I'm not a member."

Now, having just read about my willingness to chuck money into the middle of a field you might think that I would have been very ready to go to a casino. Not so; up to this point in my life the Chartered Accountant/Saturn/Adult part of me had tended to hold the upper hand and my gambling activities - apart from bad investments - had been confined to an annual flutter on the office sweepstake for the Grand National horse race.

However, some five years earlier I had become a member of one of the Casinos in Birmingham, not because of an incipient rush into the arcane rituals of the roulette wheel but because, at that time, the casino was one of the few places where I could take business associates and be sure of getting a vegetarian lunch.

It seemed like I had the answer to Jo's problem and although not greatly enthusiastic about watching people gamble away for hours on end I thought that the greater good probably lay in making myself available so that the soldier could enjoy his last night in England.

I seem to recall that the casino had some rule about wearing ties which really would have been the final straw as, at that time, I was so tired of wearing the things round my throat every day that I would do almost anything to avoid them between Friday evening and Monday morning. Furthermore, ties are almost considered to be illegal in Israel and many Israelis refuse ever to wear one - not even at their own weddings. Accordingly we went with open-necked shirts but if such a rule was in force we must have looked sufficiently respectable for I was duly admitted along with the soldier and Jo and his wife.

Always one to sample new experiences I agreed that I would change £10 and play a little - just to be sociable.

I watched the other players at the roulette table place their bets a few times. The little ball ran around the wheel making a clattering sound disproportionate to its size. My mind went back to the toy roulette wheel that my friend had had when I was about ten or eleven years old - it had always seemed such a silly game. Then I recalled the films I had seen where the roulette wheel always seemed to be rigged - could this be going on here I wondered.

Eventually I jumped off the metaphorical diving board and placed a bet - the lowest value chip I could find on the safest odds available. A twenty-five pence bet that the ball would land on a black number - did my adventuring know no limits! Well, I figured, you have to start somewhere in this game and it seemed as though I had chosen the right place as the ball *did* land on a black number and I won fifty pence as well as getting my stake money back.

I was too excited to bet on the next throw of the wheel but regained my concentration and watched a few more results before finding enough courage to venture into the arena again. I was feeling safer now; even if I lost this twenty-five pence bet I would still be ahead on the evening overall by twenty-five pence. But I didn't lose. I won and I kept on winning, on average, I suppose, about four rolls out of five for the next half an hour; never betting more than fifty pence and only straying once or twice into odds which were longer than three to one.

Just as I was getting to dreams of glory - I could already see the headlines the following day "Novice Gambler Cleans Out Casino!" - I realised what was going on. I counted the chips and found I had the equivalent of £27 in my hand which, deducting the £10 I started with, gave me a profit of £17 for the evening.

I knew that my purpose in life had nothing to do with making lots of money on a casino table and that if I kept on and tried to make the big time I would surely lose what I already had. What had happened was that the Universe had provided me with an opportunity to help someone else feel their own joy which *is* a part of my purpose and when I had done that then my investment in the fields of Warwickshire had been returned very quickly.

Whether or not I approved of the soldier gambling was not relevant; it was what he needed to do at that time and maybe he would learn something from the experience which would take him a little further on his journey.

Not wishing to hang on the excess winnings I bought a round of drinks and still had enough over to pay for the car park so that, give or take a few pence, I got home with the £12 and no more.

I sometimes wonder who picked up the money in the stone circle, whether it was one person or a number of different people and how they thought it got there but I suppose it doesn't really matter.

CHAPTER 3

JONATHON CLARK – BIOGRAPHICAL NOTE

5 June 1954	Born in London, (John Isaac Clark) at 1.05 a.m. British Summer Time, only child of Robert and Miriam Clark.
1954-1972	Childhood and education in London. Obtains respectable examination results and is head boy in final year at school.
5 November 1971	Passes driving test.
28 September 1972	Moves to Birmingham, supposedly for three years, to take a degree in Minerals Engineering.
January 1973	Realises he is totally unsuited to Minerals Engineering and obtains a place to take a degree in English the following academic year.
Summer 1973	Counsellor at a summer camp in New York State.
Summer 1974	Visits Israel. Works on a Kibbutz picking fruit. Expectations of joyful community spirit are disappointed.
Summer 1976	Graduates with a degree in English.
1976-1988	Trains as a chartered accountant with a major firm and qualifies in 1979 having passed all examinations at the first attempt. Spends nine years in various posts in industry rising to Financial Director by the age of twenty-nine.
19 December 1976	Marries Janet Elizabeth Goldstein.
December 1977	Writes "Toby Arnott Drops Back In."
13 March 1978	First son born, Robin David.

15

The Barefoot Accountant

26 January 1980	Second son born, Daniel Alexander.
18 January 1983	Third son born, Joel Simon.
July 1984	The "Toby Arnott Poems" are published.
September 1986	Visits Findhorn Foundation for the first time. Discovers the joy of community which he had searched for in vain on kibbutz.
Autumn 1986	Life in turmoil as he tries to recapture the joy he felt at Findhorn in his everyday life. Very close to burn-out. Plans to leave home and job to move to Findhorn but pulls back at the last moment.
1987	Temporary respite from traumas of late 1986. Begins to realise that "escaping to Findhorn" is not the answer. Joy is something which is carried within the individual - wherever they may be.
August 1988	Marriage ends as partners' desired lifestyles have diverged irreconcilably. Lives with Jane Ann Hooper and her daughter, Kate Crabtree.
31 October 1988	Leaves employed position and works independently running seminars, carrying out business consultancy and advising on investment products. More time is now available for "being" rather than "doing" - although both are necessary.
1988-89	Learns spiritual lessons in the most unlikely places - Euston station, for example. Also in the local snooker hall where he pots more balls by hitting them gently than by hitting them hard and on the tennis court where his coach insists that he has to "give the ball room and let it come to you."

Still living in Birmingham after seventeen years. |

Jonathon Clark - Biographical Note

19 May 1989	Changes name by Deed Poll to Jonathon Clark.
July-September 1989	Writes "The Barefoot Accountant".
November 1989	Opens "Hoopers" with Jane - a small bookshop in Birmingham.
March 1990	Writes the last chapter of "The Barefoot Accountant."

CHAPTER 4

PAY AS YOU EARN

In the recession years of the early and mid-nineteen-eighties British companies found themselves with enormous problems - not just in trying to make a profit but also in their day to day cash management; it is generally believed that far more businesses fail for want of good cash management than for want of profit.

To a large extent this is a reflection of the notion of "Creative Accounting" - profit is seen as a commodity which can be massaged, negotiated, smoothed or generally moulded according to the preference of the Board of Directors whereas the cash in the bank is an undisputed figure - or is it?

As a sharp young Financial Director I had experienced the rough and tumble of learning the art of cash management and followed the general principle that we tried to get our customers to pay us as quickly as possible whilst stringing out our suppliers for as long as possible. Indeed, I still recall the confusion into which one of my Managing Directors was thrown when he was congratulated by the Group Chairman on having four months creditors outstanding i.e. we were taking an *average* of four months to pay our suppliers.

He didn't know whether to accept the compliment with grace or to show the Chairman the list of suppliers who would no longer trade with us and the production line which was consequently grinding to a halt for want of material. The Chairman, however, had his own priorities and maybe the conflicts would have been fewer if we had sat and talked with each other rather than see the whole process as an adversarial game even though we were all, nominally, part of the same organisation.

Creditors - people to whom we owed money - fell into various categories such as employees, suppliers and the tax authorities. At the worst of the recession in 1982-84 it was still considered the final straw when employees were not paid on time; there was a sort of understanding that once you could not pay the staff then the game was up and the liquidator came in.

Suppliers and tax authorities were a different matter, though.   In an effort to stem the tide of insolvencies the Inland Revenue were prepared to accept all sorts of deals outside the statutory arrangements which state that Income Tax deducted from an employee's salary must be paid over no later than the 19th. of the month following the month in which it has been deducted.

By 1986 the recession had eased a little and, accordingly, the Inland Revenue set about restoring companies to the straight and narrow path from which it had given tacit permission to stray during the previous few years.

During that year I was challenged most months by the Inland Revenue to improve our payment terms although by the standards of the time and district we were not doing badly.   The sticking point, however, was the fact that the

Company Budget had been set on the assumption that we would always take two months credit. For example, if we deducted tax from our employees' salaries in February then the money should have been paid over to the Inland Revenue by 19th. March but following the practice we had adopted we would have held it until at least the 1st. April.

The crucial point here was that our Balance Sheet looked a lot better - about £100,000 better - if the money was sitting in our bank account rather than having been paid to the Inland Revenue thus depleting our Cash Balance or, rather, increasing our overdraft. Also, it was embarrassing to show this variance against budget and being a rising and aspiring young star I was trying very hard to show the company's best profile in the accounts which I submitted each month.

I managed to stall the Inland Revenue throughout 1986 with the excuse that I could do nothing until we had a new budget and that as our monthly accounts were circulated to the Bank I felt it important to preserve the company's reputation - to say nothing of my own!

Come the budgetting season and, naturally, there were many more weighty matters pressing on my mind than the Inland Revenue with the result that I forgot to adjust the assumptions about payment periods. Our new budget for 1987 therefore showed the same expectation - that we would take two months to pay our PAYE (Pay As You Earn) and NI (National Insurance) despite the statute and my half-promise that we would in future pay on time.

What we did do, however, in response to continued pressure from the Inland Revenue, was to agree to pay on the last day of the following month i.e. about twelve days late. By doing this however, we could count the cheque as having been paid in the following month since we dated it say, 1 March instead of 28 February. Our balance sheet remained intact and the Inland Revenue could justifiably claim to have collected the cheque in the month in which the cheque was due - even if it was twelve days late.

Yes, I know, the same cash was being counted as being in the possession of two different people at the same time - a practice known as "window-dressing" and which has been a widespread business practice for some years. Which is why I finished the second paragraph of this story with some uncertainty over whether cash in the bank was an undisputed figure.

Eventually I got tired of this game or, to put it another

way, my (Chartered Accountant's) conscience began to prick too much for comfort.

Whilst the 19th. March had come and gone and we planned to make our next payment on 31st. March but dated 1 April in respect of our February PAYE I felt the time had arrived to make a gesture of friendship to the Inland Revenue.   As it happened I was due to go away for a long weekend on Thursday 26 March but left instructions that the cheque, for about £100,000 was to be paid on Friday 27th. March.

When I returned the following Tuesday my first call of the morning was to ensure that the cheque had been paid, which it duly had.

My second call was to the credit control department to see how our collections were doing for the month of March which closed that day.   The supervisor, a woman who had worked at the company for almost twenty years and who claimed to "have seen it all" was still recovering from the post which had been received the previous day and which had included a cheque for £200,000 from our largest customer who *always* paid on the same day each month and whose next cheque had not been due until 5 April.

The credit controller could not understand it but, nevertheless, was very pleased that she had collected so much cash during the month.

Of course, when we submitted our accounts for March the Cash Balance in our Balance Sheet was £100,000 *better* than we would have expected had we continued with our previous practice rather than being £100,000 *worse* as I had planned.

There was a line of thought amongst my more prosaic colleagues which said that, had we kept to our usual practice with the Inland Revenue our Balance Sheet would have been not just £100,000 better but £200,000 better than expected. For my own part I just wondered why our customer should have picked that particular month to pay early.

Of course, our customer reverted to his normal practice (which were the terms agreed between us) the following month but I continued to ensure that our taxes were paid on time; although no such spectacular "co-incidences" occurred again who is to say what misfortunes might have befallen us had we gone back to our old ways?

CHAPTER 5

TOBY ARNOTT DROPS BACK IN

Our story starts in Oxford, one July,
With Toby Arnott blinking at the sky -
Still drunk from parties held to celebrate
His elevation to the rank of "Graduate."
But underneath his drunkenness there lies
A realisation that this paradise
Of part-time intellectual stimulation
And frequent anti-Nixon demonstration
Is at an end and must now be replaced
With something more conventional - more straightlaced.
What likelier course but that a French degree
Should lead its owner to accountancy?
It might be thought improbable at first
That anyone with Toby Arnott's thirst
For University's indiscipline
Should contemplate a lifetime spent within
The confines of a tie and pinstripe suit;
It is, indeed, unlikely that this route
Would have been that of our protagonist
Had he been able to disperse the mist
Of indecision which made everything unclear
When looking for a suitable career.
An entry into finance was suggested
By Toby's father - feeling he had vested
Sufficient wealth in Toby's education
To feed and clothe three-quarters of the nation.
So, finding Toby had no set design,
He said, "Why don't you see a friend of mine?"
He's Senior Partner in a City firm -
Pay him a visit at the end of term.
His plate is clear to any passer-by
'Chartered Accountants - Reed Galbraith and Dye.' "
Toby agreed to keep his father quiet
And so prevent another family riot
Not dreaming that he ever would accept
A job for which he felt he was inept.
Then, in late autumn, when the days grew colder
He cut his hair to just below the shoulder,
Put on the suit he wore for all exams
And headed for the smoke and traffic jams.

23

The Barefoot Accountant

Remembering nineteenth-century images
Of draughty and archaic offices
Toby experienced genuine surprise
When going into Reed Galbraith and Dye's.
The thick pile carpet covering the floors
Fit snugly under automatic doors.
He signed in and the blonde receptionist
Glanced quickly down the Senior Partner's list
Of visitors, "Yes, Mr. Arnott, fine.
Please go on up to room eighteen-o-nine."
The Senior Partner lived in regal style
With mohair suit, Havanas and a smile
He kept especially for his wealthiest client.
To Toby he looked ruthless and defiant.
"I've not much time," he barked, "but tell me why
You want to work for Reed Galbraith and Dye."
Toby had found out what he ought to say
From older friends who'd travelled the same way
And though his speech was free from contradiction
The partner sensed a lack of firm conviction.
Although he'd interviewed some candidates
Far keener, he applied the rule which states
That intuition often is much better
Than judging things according to the letter.
The urge to offer him a job was strong
Because he'd known Toby's father for so long.
And so, for no more complicated reason,
Toby was asked to join them the next season.
A major inconsistency appeared
For, long before our hero had been geared
To Marx and Lenin and to Che Guevara,
He'd worn gold rings - his sister a tiara.
He found this background difficult to lose
And, much as Toby would have liked to choose
A peasant's life in jeans and cheesecloth shirt,
The thought that real poverty could hurt
Eventually won so Toby said -
Remembering statements from the bank in red -
"I'm interested - but I'd like to hear
What I will earn in my first working year."
"A thousand pounds and all exam fees paid -
In three years time your future will be made!"
The prophecy was cast and nine months later
Toby arrived in London looking straighter
Than many of his friends would have believed.

Toby Arnott Drops Back In

They felt they had been drastically deceived
To hear that one of Oxford's bright young thinkers
Was set to run for forty years in blinkers.
But, clinging to his radical ideals,
Like Jacob clutching hold of Esau's heels,
He vowed to bring all dirty deals to light
Supplanting what was wrong with what was right.
On Toby's first assignment - a large audit -
Everyone kept protesting they were bored, it
Took a major effort to survive
From nine o'clock, through lunch, to half past five.
He learnt about commercial cut and thrust,
How never to take anyone on trust
And how ambition drowns all thought of lust.

For many months Toby recalled his days
In Oxford and the many different ways
He would have gone if he could choose again
Truly he found accountancy a strain.

But, gradually his new environment
Enveloped him and he is now intent
On qualifying - then he wants to try
For partnership in Reed Galbraith and Dye.
Explaining Toby's changeability
Would take a thesis in psychology.
Suffice to say that, having once dropped out,
He's dropped back in and cleared his mind of doubt.
Toby is learning to forget the past -
He's trapped within the real world, at last.

CHAPTER 6

COMPANY CARS

When I was twenty-six the most important short term goal in my career was to drive a company car. This, I had been led to believe, was the ultimate measure of worth.

And I was not alone in my ambition.

A further advantage of driving a company car - which was important for me - was that I would not have the "worry" of owning one. Whenever it needed servicing or repairing I could simply book it into the garage, give a lofty command to fix whatever was wrong and not concern myself with the cost.

Garages, of course, love dealing with company cars as the customer rarely argues about the final bill! This is a good example of the different attitude we are prone to take when spending someone else's money rather than our own. It is also an example of not wanting to take responsibility for what is going on in our lives - and I use the word "our" justifiably as I know many other people who have behaved in the same way.

When I did reach the position where I had a company car I was not only relieved of the capital and maintenance costs of motoring but was also allowed to charge all my petrol costs to the company, business and private.

I used to wonder why I drove so many more miles once I had a company car when the nature of my job had hardly changed. After a little thought the answer was quite clear. It now cost me absolutely nothing to make a journey by car and so I would travel on "pleasure" quite unnecessarily. Would the visits I made to friends in different parts of the country have been of a better quality if I had made fewer of them? Were they really necessary or was I just contributing to the traffic jams that seem to have increased so much in recent years.

It seems to me that the increase in traffic jams is a logical application of Parkinson's Law. As roads are opened and fill with cars and lorries so decisions are made to build more roads rather than examining just why they got full in the first place. Would it not be more useful to consider changing our ideas about business travel rather than tearing up another swathe of countryside?

This issue comes to mind more strongly in the early Spring each year. The income tax payable on company cars is dependent on the size of the engine, the age of the car and the number of business miles travelled each year. Thus, by February, with the end of the tax year beckoning on 5th April company car drivers become very aware of the mileage which they have driven since last April.

This is not an issue to the hardened salesman driving 40,000 miles in a year but, to someone who has the possibility of reducing the income tax due in respect of his car by one third if he exceeds 2,500 business miles or of halving his bill by motoring more than 18,000 business miles, the number of miles driven before Easter can become a significant influence on business activity. Managers in Plymouth suddenly remember a customer in Newcastle who needs a visit whilst the clamouring to use the Shuttle Air Service from Manchester to London is deferred as executives burst into self righteousness and talk about "saving the company money by using the car."

Many seasoned company car users hovering around these cut-off points of 2,500 miles and 18,000 miles will regard it as sensible tax planning to drive the extra miles in March, regardless of the business logic. Many of the more senior, desk-bound executives who commute each day by train to their office struggle to drive 2,500 business miles in a year and so the motorways start to clog with wealthy men making journeys of questionable necessity in order to reduce their tax bill by almost as much as a student might receive by way of grant in an entire twelvemonth.

Maybe I stretch the point a little in asking you to visualise a motorway packed full of Daimlers and Rolls Royces but I have seen many examples of men on high incomes going to great lengths to escape paying income tax.

Foremost amongst these was the executive for whom I was making a return to the Inland Revenue about his benefits received from the company. I had entered on the form that his annual business mileage was at the standard rate - between 2,500 and 18,000 business miles - and pointed this out to him as I took him through the information which would form the basis for his income tax assessment.

He said that he always claimed for business use in excess of 18,000 miles and that I should change the form to reflect this. Since I had all the mileages of the cars written down I protested that this was surely incorrect as his three year old car had travelled 56,000 miles and I supposed he had done more than 2,000 private miles in that time.

He claimed this to be irrelevant and even went outside to check the mileage. He stuck to his point, weaving a whole series of suppositions which we could put to the Inland Revenue in the event of a dispute including the possibility that he had used his wife's car at the weekends - which we both knew was not the case!

It intrigued me that a man with a good income could go to such lengths to withhold his tax. What were the underlying issues for him, I wondered? Where did the resentment come from at handing over money to the tax authorities? The same man had once put forward the theory that companies that made profits should not pay tax but companies that made losses should pay as a deterrent against future poor performances. Perhaps he was using a similar rationale with the Inland Revenue on the grounds that he could put the money to better use than them.

Maybe he regarded the whole system of tax on company cars as unfair; the atmosphere was too heated to explore the issue in any depth but I did not change the information on the form. Whether or not he appealed against his assessment I don't know.

Come to think of it, the ancient Chinese doctors were, I believe, only remunerated if their patients were well and had money deducted if patients died. They even had to hang lanterns outside their surgeries when a patient had died so that prospective patients might take the warning.

Few and far between are men like one Managing Director for whom I worked who decided he didn't want to pay as much income tax and so declined the offer of a Ford Granada 2.3L when he was appointed to the job. Instead, he chose a Vauxhall Cavalier 1.8CD and the reactions of the other Directors were generally not so much of admiration as of grave concern lest their own cars were downgraded when due for replacement.

All of us, somewhere, have people to whom we do not want to pay money or give our energy and the Inland Revenue represents an easy target for us to erect in order to project such feelings. Oak trees are less discriminating about the people and creatures to whom they offer shade and shelter; the sun is totally open in its willingness to nourish life with its warmth yet we humans run around holding on to our money and our love as though, should we give them away, we would never receive any more.

When we give we receive as is demonstrated in some of the other stories in this book.

The status afforded by company cars can have far reaching effects beyond one's individual actions. I once drove a Ford Escort for a couple of months and made my declaration to the Inland Revenue based on an engine size of 1600cc., which was in line with the badge on the back of the car. A year later, when I was in conversation with someone elsewhere in the group of companies who was compiling some information for a report, I found out that the registration documents in his possession showed an engine capacity of 1300cc; a different - and lower - tax bracket altogether.

We tracked back through the previous drivers of the car and realised that one particularly status conscious driver - no longer with the company - had very probably changed the badge on the back of the car to impress those around her and her actions had almost cost me £100 in income tax! I also was now able to understand why the car had seemed to perform so badly for one with an engine of 1600cc.

Company cars, which are supposed to be either a tool of the trade or awarded as recognition of the seniority of an employee and are therefore meant to generate a positive feeling are, in my experience, the biggest source of aggravation, resentment and jealousy in many businesses. The case of the changed badge quoted above is one of the more extreme examples of the unwarranted importance which company cars assume but the man hours spent by employees discussing the relative merits of four or five speed gear boxes, sunroofs, metallic paint and the finer points of the "in-car entertainment" system (the simple "car radio" is a thing of the past) would stretch the credulity of anyone who has never worked in that level of management.

The growth of company cars is a relatively British phenomenon. Other countries do not seem to award them with nearly the same readiness and having now almost exhausted the possibility of luring someone into a job by means of offering a car - it really is regarded as standard in so many cases - there are ever more novel ways of impressing the prospective employee. The idea of a high salary and no perks seems to be a forgotten option in the UK; whatever the level of perks it is still the absolute figure on the payroll which can cause havoc with existing salary structures and so various ways are found of clouding the issue.

Company Cars

Subscriptions to Health Clubs, free life assurance, free use of the company villa; all are examples of ways in which the employee's life becomes so enmeshed with the company that there is a great likelihood for an addiction to the company to ensue.   The employee finds it increasingly difficult to move to alternative employment where he will be cocooned in the same way and so stays with the same company.   That, of course, is the whole idea of the "corporate compensation strategy", but in itself is faulty because it harbours the potential for employees becoming stale; if the employer were to risk the employee moving who knows what fresh impetus would come from the replacement?

I have mentioned briefly the fact that cars are awarded as a piece of business equipment or as a straightforward perk; both areas open up the proverbial can of worms when the capital expenditure proposals are put to the Board.

Where cars are awarded as recognition of seniority all sorts of preferences and prejudices come to the fore such as the relative merits of accountants and engineers and if the Managing Director has his original skills in one of these functions then, despite all his training in impartiality and objectiveness, he may find it difficult to *appear* to make a fair decision even if the actual decision is sound.   What is almost certain is that aggrieved employees will assume that he is guilty of all sorts of prejudices even if he is not.

Fear of loss and fear of change are emotions which are responsible for many bad business decisions.   In the area of company cars - and other perks - it is often assumed that if the company does not let Fred have a car then he will join another company down the road.   The fear blocks the possibility that there may be another employee waiting in the wings who could do the job better than Fred and if Fred is the sort of chap who would decide which company he wants to work for based solely on the question of a company car does the company really want him?   On the other hand, if Fred doesn't think enough of himself to obtain the market rate or package for the job is he really the sort of person the company wants?

Such questions are rarely as simple as they appear at first.

Some years ago there was almost a national outcry when people in the Labour Party muttered an intention about abolishing the tax relief on mortgages.   The hatches were battened down in the middle class towns in the South of England and hand grenades were prepared for throwing at

31

any Socialist who passed within fifty miles. Yet, as we enter the nineteen-nineties the real value of that tax relief has been eroded to a fraction of its value fifteen years ago by the falling tax rates and spiralling house prices.

One could hardly suggest making it illegal for companies to provide cars for their employees and, whilst the tax levied on company cars has increased, it is still to the considerable financial advantage of the employee to receive such a benefit. However, a further steady increase in the taxation of company cars might begin to dismantle a system which consumes enormous financial and administrative resources in many different parts of the economy. What is needed, in my view, is for some visionary Boards of Directors to have the courage to stop playing this particular game, to get off the dizzy roundabout and put the responsibility for personal transport back with the individual.

Had I never had a company car I could be accused of wishing to see the end of them through jealousy but that is not the case. I have been through the process and have experienced a whole range of feelings about them.

When I put the keys in the ignition of my first company car in June 1982 I was thrilled and assumed I would never own another car until I retired. Over the next six years I drove a number of increasingly luxurious cars with more and more sophisticated equipment, the presence of which was, in truth, marginal to my real needs.

The much sought after sun roof can actually be a rather dubious blessing. One feels obliged to use it in hot weather and yet having the sun beat down on your head as you cruise along the motorway is not the healthiest of conditions under which to drive. Electric windows are notorious for jamming open after you have put your money in the slot to activate the car wash and whilst central locking is very convenient when it works it has a habit of going wrong (or at least did on one otherwise reliable car I drove) so that the car is inadvertently left unlocked.

I never thought I would get as much pleasure from driving a plain Ford Escort again. It is one more area in which I am able to make a decision about what happens in my life without having to conform to "company policy."

One of the more insane aspects of "company policy" prevalent in much of British Industry is that company cars should be British. Quite apart from the fact that this undermines the concept of a global economy there are some crazy side effects. At one point, I took delivery of a new Vauxhall

Carlton which conformed with the dictum of being a British Car - the first thing I did was to remove the label from the windscreen which said "Made in West Germany." I'm afraid I never did - and still don't - understand the logic which said that a car where many of the components were made in West Germany but the final assembly of which took place in England could be called either "British" *or* "German".

I am glad to have left such madness behind me.

CHAPTER 7

ANOTHER WAY OF DOING IT

One of the companies of which I was Finance Director was situated in a particularly grim part of the West Midlands. The factory was built in the nineteen-thirties and still carried a feeling of the depression of how I imagine that time must have been.

The road into the factory was crumbling as lorry after lorry stormed over it. Verbal communication inside the buildings was almost impossible against a raucous background of metal being melted, welded and cut. This made little difference to the advancement of these industrial processes as, for the most part, they required little discussion. Iron and steel entered the plant at one end and emerged at the other end after being fashioned by machinery which had been patched and repaired for the last forty years to the point where a few nuts and bolts might be all that remained of the equipment which had been proudly installed in the late nineteen-forties.

Craftsmanship and the skill of the artisan were little in evidence and the casual observer might well have been excused for thinking he had stumbled into one of the industrial museums which have been constructed in the area and which are vaunted as the sort of tourist attraction that will transform the local manufacturing based economy into a service based economy.

For many of the workers there seemed to be a depressing inevitability about the daily trudge into the factory; this was only emphasised by the laughter which lit their faces as they stood by the time clock eagerly anticipating the moment when the final minute of the working day had elapsed and they could punch their card - a ticket to re-enter the outside world.

Perhaps, though, I was seeing my own unhappiness reflected in their faces. It is fair to say that we in the offices created little opportunity to talk with the factory workers and if the annual set pieces such as the Christmas dinner did manage to bring people together then it seemed to be a rather imperfect union with communication lapsing again a few days later.

If life in the factory, where you could boil in the summer and freeze in the winter, was a setting which did not provide the most fertile soil for the fulfilment of human potential then the offices were just as barren but the disease manifested in different ways.

Instead of blaming the old machinery for breaking down and making life difficult the computer became the scapegoat. Or customers who refused to pay. Or suppliers who kept telephoning for money. Or, most frequently, "the company" - a suitably anonymous label for an entity which, although composed entirely of human beings, was viewed as a monster responsible for misery in the life of any employee who was looking for something to blame apart from himself.

For all the composite misery that might be felt hanging over the site, little pockets of goodness could be found and some traditions which had been started in the more relaxed economic conditions of the nineteen-sixties survived the swashbuckling sabres of successive managements who believed that cutting every cost in sight was the quickest way of turning a company round from loss to profit.

One of these traditions was a recognition that the company was part of the surrounding town and a charitable deed had been executed some years previously whereby £750, supplemented by income tax recovered from the Inland Revenue, was distributed to local charities.

Quite how the decisions had been reached over who should benefit I do not know but when I first arrived in the job I simply kept the begging letters received in the year and handed them over to the Personnel Manager for a recommendation. Frankly, in the crisis in which the company found itself in the mid-eighties, I looked at the whole affair as a bit of a nuisance and in the terms in which I later came to understand money, the cheques may have been written but there was no energy flowing with them. If you are going to give something to someone then do it with feeling!

Still, even this was better than the remark made by one old boss of mine who refused to give any money to a local charity as "we couldn't afford it." I too may have at one time been sceptical about the platitude that only when we give do we receive but have now experienced enough incidents - some are recorded in the chapter called "Moneyflow" - to know that this is true.

How many times in our lives do we distance ourselves from financial transactions to which we pretend we are a party? We are urged to pay for gas or electricity by standing order to smooth the payments and make it easier to budget but by doing so we may well lose the feeling of actually consuming large quantities of energy to heat our homes in the winter. There is nothing quite like a large bill for gas received on a bright March day to make us appreciate the reality that we have been burning gas for three months in such quantities that we might consider wearing an additional sweater instead next year.

We are offered an anaesthetic and take it thankfully. Many people in a job lose total contact with their money; their salary is paid in through a bank giro transfer and immediately disappears in a clutch of direct debits. The pleasure of receiving a payslip to explain how my large salary had been paid into the bank was nothing to the joy of the week's wages in cash received for doing a holiday job or the cheques with my name written on them that come to me now and which I take to the bank myself.

We can lose contact with money in other ways - by doing things for the wrong reasons. Some years ago I also covenanted to pay money to a charity account from which I could write vouchers to individual causes - the reason for doing this was that income tax could be recovered and so more money was available for distribution.

However, I came to feel that the single large payment made once a year from my bank account was a burden and that, once I had made the payment, I would often forget that there was money lying around in the charity account and which needed to be passed on further. When I wrote the vouchers I had little of the feeling of giving as all the energy had been transmitted in that large annual payment. Better, for me, to give a little less money by not recovering the tax but to feel each gift as an act of love rather than the annual payment as a millstone and its eventual distribution as a chore. Who knows, I might have finished up giving more but not have felt under such a strain.

The distribution of the company charity money offered an opportunity for getting people together and, one year, I asked Brian, our personnel manager, if he would like to be part of a group which took responsibility for distributing the money. It was not, I emphasised, to be a Committee, which had also been tried, but an exploration of something a little different. He agreed and the two of us together with Barry, one of the production managers, Sharon from Wages and two foremen, Albert and Dilip gathered in my office one Friday morning.

Instead of adopting the usual arrangement for a meeting of sitting round a table where we obscure much of ourselves from our colleagues we sat in a circle with no table to separate us. We began the meeting by introducing ourselves, and saying a little about the work we did and what we enjoyed about it. Each member of the group had been asked whether they would like to help disperse the money and had agreed and although most of us knew each of the others by sight this was an occasion where we could create an environment in which we might know each other a little better. Perhaps that is also a purpose of business; perhaps that is a higher purpose of business than achieving a financial goal, to find ways in which we can come to know each other and ourselves better.

I then outlined the position. For some reason tax had not been reclaimed in an earlier year and neither had all of the money been spent so that the total amount in the bank was £1,358. It was desirable, although not compulsory, that the money benefit local, rather than national, charities who would be able to connect more directly with the company.

For those who have suffered in meetings from incessant talking and discussion, argument and debate, accusation and recrimination, I recommend that you look at the option of not talking. A minute's silence can produce answers where three hours of discussion have generated anger and despondency.

Wc closed our eyes and were quiet. I asked that we find in our hearts the people in our locality who needed money. I can't recall how long we sat in silence, probably no more than five minutes but I felt a sense of peace was among us and, for my own recommendation, saw a swimming pool in my mind which meant absolutely nothing!

When we talked again my five colleagues had quite clear ideas of where the money should go and I asked that we should hold my uncertainty as an anonymous beneficiary for the present whose identity would become clear in time. All that remained for this meeting was to decide how much money should go to each charity. Could we, I asked, each name an amount for the charity we had nominated and see how much the bill totalled.

Having been bred in the tradition of negotiation and bargaining I was assuming that we would inevitably want to spend, for argument's sake, £2,000 and that this would then have to be cut back by way of compromise. Every year we went through this exercise with our budget - lopping £20,000 off repairs or £30,000 off marketing. Such procedure seemed to be the norm in commercial life and we were given a precedent to follow when we heard of government depart-ments having to follow the same path with the Chancellor; £5,000,000 off Health, £6,000,000 off Education. The figures were larger but the principle was the same.

However, although this group was exploring a different way of making decisions I had forgotten the potency of such methods - perhaps because I had read or heard about them more than I had experienced them myself. With little debate each member named his charity and suggested a figure. Each time, the rest of the group gave a nod of general approval that the gift was of an appropriate size or discussed the matter briefly, perhaps guiding us to the upper or lower end of a proposed range.

As this was going on I realised that the swimming pool in my mind's eye was the pool at a school for handicapped children in Birmingham which was hired out for children's parties. The school was very near to a factory in Birming-ham which was also part of our company. "Local" clearly included parts that might be forgotten as they were not on the main site.

Barry named two charities, the rest of us one each and, after we all voiced our figures Brian, who had been jotting the figures down, totalled them. They came to £1,300 and there was a rather startled guffaw from all of us, so accustomed were we to assuming that every decision had to be made by compromise. We were not used to the joy of consensus.

The meeting closed and we agreed to contact the charities in order to arrange a visit.

A week later we met again and spent the morning visiting the charities not only to take them a cheque but also to spend some time with the people involved with them. We actually learned something about what happened in the charity and the charity workers learned a little about what went on in our working lives in the industrial sector.

It was not just money that was changing hands. The money provided a vehicle for communication, for learning about other people and for experiencing parts of the world with which we might not normally have come into contact.

The stories that we heard of the mentally handicapped, the work of a local Salvation Army hostel, a little girl suffering from a terminal illness all brought a sense of proportion to the work that we did in our daily lives. There was, indeed, life beyond the balance sheet and the charity group, having completed its work, disbanded.

It was, for me, a taste of the way in which business *can* be conducted; gently, with care and love. When such qualities are present it is no wonder that decisions can be reached with unanimity and that there are sufficient resources for everyone.

CHAPTER 8

TOBY ARNOTT – ARTICLED CLERK

When Toby signed his articles he thought
That he was, metaphorically, caught
Within a cage, the doors of which were closed -
Escape was very doubtful he supposed.
Although a disillusioned soldier who,
When sick of all that he is going through,
May purchase freedom Toby would not buy
His liberty from Reed Galbraith and Dye.
The firm had made a written pledge, now he
Must serve them well and learn accountancy.
Atrocious students might be asked to leave
But Toby could not make himself achieve
His freedom by deliberately failing
Exams which seemed, to him, to be plain sailing.
Though these exams brought many to their knees
Toby was bright and took them at his ease.
An Oxford French degree can't guarantee
Success in something needing numeracy
But Toby had an excellent I.Q.
Which he believed would always see him through.
His early days, spent fetching cups of tea,
Were tedious and long but, gradually,
Toby began a gradual advance -
Another batch of graduate debutantes
Entered the firm and Toby was no more
Required to carry out each menial chore.
No longer did he think that double entry
Was soixant-neuf as practised by the gentry.
And though he managed to adjust his mind
To help keep wealthy pockets warmly lined
And didn't shout or even once protest
His student days had left a strong bequest.
For, in his mind, there often nagged away
The thought that many are worse off than they
Who sit in comfortable, soft-cushioned chairs
Ruling with sharp commands and piercing stares.
These doubts rose to the surface on the date
That Toby saw his brother graduate;

Toby Arnott – Articled Clerk

He heard in Oxford over that weekend
The story of an old and trusted friend
Who thought his city life a dismal failure
So packed his bags and hitchhiked to Australia.
"But what's he going to do when he arrives?"
Asked Toby, recollecting how their lives
Had once had much in common, now it seemed
As though such comradeship had all been dreamed.
He listened as the friend who brought the news
Replied, "Well, man, I guess he'll just hang loose,
It's cool to live like that - I spent a year
Bummin' around in Tunis and Tangier."
Toby had quite forgotten this strange creed
Of carefree living but perceived a need
To throw away the shackles he was wearing
And live his life without so much as caring
Whether the price of shares went up or down
Mentally he was halfway out of town.
Toby resolved that, once he'd qualified,
He'd break away; and though he might have tried
For partnership - at times he'd though he would -
He'd had enough; maybe he'd do some good,
Float round the world, perhaps he'd even go
To live on a kibbutz, do VSO
Or simply stand and watch the river flow.
His final year of Articles dragged on -
How Toby wished that it would soon be gone -
Until the summer brought examinations;
September brought results and expectations.
Though Toby didn't think he was the best
He felt he'd adequately passed the test.
Confidently he slit the envelope
And there he found - beyond his wildest hope,
That, overall, he'd taken second place;
A worried frown flickered across his face.
He'd won a prize - he would be called a star -
Everyone would expect him to go far.
On Monday morning he was asked to see
One of the partners who immediately
Took from his desk a cheque he'd drawn on Coutts
And said "I understand the Institute's
Awarded you a prize - excellent news!
Three hundred pounds should buy a first class cruise,
We have a client who runs a shipping line,
I hear the weather in the Med is fine.

41

The Barefoot Accountant

This is a token of congratulation
In recognition of your dedication.
We'll give you instantaneous promotion
(The firm expects professional devotion)
We'll also give you a substantial rise -
We're proud of you at Reed Galbraith and Dye's.
Just sign this contract here and we'll enjoy
A celebration lunch at the Savoy!"
Said Toby, "Thanks a lot, that all sounds fine,"
Forgetting he'd intended to resign.
These offers seem too good; I guess I'll stay
Conjectured Toby Arnott, A.C.A.

CHAPTER 9

THE LAW OF BUSINESS BALANCE

When an incident occurs in our lives and we fail to learn from it then it is a certainty that the same incident will pop up again in a different costume to offer us another opportunity to learn the lesson. If we are hurt by the incident then we will simply carry on getting hurt by that situation until we learn to handle it properly.

Despite my calling to deal with the issue of money and, in particular, other people's money, this does not mean that I have cracked my own money issues. I don't have lashings of the stuff hidden away, either under the mattress or in a Swiss Bank Acount and, given the principle that we teach what we most need to learn, then it is my belief that by helping other people with the issues raised by money I am actually healing myself in relation to money.

Over the years I have been lured time and again by the promise of material wealth only to find that just as I was reaching the crock of gold somebody had moved the end of the rainbow. Pinned to my wall is a quote attributed to John Ruskin. I don't know which work contains it but it was also pinned to the wall behind the chair of a former boss of mine and it is worth setting down here, I think:

"It's unwise to pay too much but it's worse to pay too little.

When you pay too much you lose a little money, that is all.

When you pay too little, you sometimes lose everything, because the thing you bought was incapable of doing the thing it was bought to do.

The common law of business balance prohibits paying a little and getting a lot - it can't be done.

If you deal with the lowest bidder, it is well to add something for the risk you run. And if you do that, you will have enough for something better."

Quite.

Having had some money for my twenty-first birthday I took it in search of a home in London's West End. I lighted on a shop where goods appeared to be coming across the counter at remarkable low prices compared with the value attributed them by the auctioneer. I cannot now recall the exact details but I do know I paid £10 for a watch which was supposed to be worth £50 - or whatever - and, having then decided to check it out with a reputable jeweller found it was worth only £5. Ruskin, had I but read you then.

I was mortified of course to find that my special birthday money had disappeared and that I had got, according to the jeweller, a most unreliable watch. I returned to the shop jeweller, a most unreliable watch. I returned to the shop where I had bought it and remonstrated with the auctioneer but I may as well have saved my breath.

Well, I didn't learn about "the common law of business balance" from that incident because some years later, when my bank balance was a little higher than it needed to be and I was climbing the Executive Ladder another incident came my way. In that ascendant position it seemed to me that I should start to collect a portfolio of shares.

I had heard that such possessions were the natural accompaniment to the Company Car. Even though one might not leave the share certificates on the dashboard for public display it was good form to have such a topic in one's head for conversation at business lunches and dinner parties.

Sure enough, my attention began to be drawn to the share tipping circulars and columns of the Sunday newspapers. Despite all I had learned in my accountancy training about portfolio analysis (the theory that long term gain will be greater by putting money into a range of investments, thereby spreading the risk, rather than putting all one's money into one company) I thought that I could beat the system.

It was, therefore, only a matter of time before I found a suitably doomed company in which to invest and the £1500 which I invested in 1984 is now worth about £150.

Never have I advised a client to invest all his surplus money into a single company, let alone a high risk, Australian oil company. But all the tipsters said it had "excellent recovery prospects" - a sure euphemism for the fact that it was bombed out and going lower.

Still I didn't learn and my situation was parallel to the demise of the Australian cricketer Andrew Hilditch on the 1985 tour f England. Hilditch was an inveterate hooker of the bouncer and was dismissed a number of times by Ian Botham as he rose to the bait of a shortpitched ball. Even though Hilditch had almost certainly watched the extra fieldsman being put in position behind him he would still hook the ball into their eager hands - and fall for exactly the same ploy in the second innings! Not content with having lost money in Asia Oils and Minerals I was attracting the same situation two years later.

This time £1000 went down the drain as a result of a telephone call from a firm of so-called stockbrokers in London who were marketing shares in a company developing electronic catheters. Yes, really. After I had agreed to buy the shares over the 'phone - I believe such an agreement constituted a legally binding contract - the voice on the other end thanked me for my faith in the company. A shudder ran down my spine and instead of the trebling in value over the next five months which he had promised I found the shares to be worthless by the following Spring.

At one point I did make a profit on a small number of shares - about £150 - only to discover that I had lost the share certificates in the middle of a whole host of obsolete files and it took three months for a duplicate to be issued and the sale proceeds of the shares to reach my bank account. I think I finally learned my lesson as far as committing large funds are concerned after that incident - I have a clean sheet in the last three years - but that did not stop me pursuing the possibility of accruing large sums of money from litte effort - Reader's Digest is a case in point.

In the summer of 1988 I received a mailshot from Reader's Digest - the latest in a long line - assuring me that I had successfully completed the first two rounds in their latest Prize Draw. If I filled in the necessary coupons and agreed to take a year's subscription - 20% off at £13.67 - then I would be eligible to be entered in the draw in which the first prize was £100,000.

My mind went around the issue something like this: "I know it seems pointless, spending £13.67 on something I'm not likely to read but I might win £100,000 and then I will have more than recouped my stake. On the other hand if I don't take out the subscription then I certainly won't win £100,000 and I'll always be wondering. . ."

I expressed these doubts to Robin, my eldest son, then aged ten, who encouraged me, with a glint in his eye. It was not typical of his behaviour to encourage me in such a venture and I wondered whether he might have an insight which I didn't so I decided to write out the cheque.

Of course, I didn't win the money. I have written elsewhere in this book about my predisposition towards handling other people's money due to my astrological make-up. Saturn in the eighth house can also bring restrictions on winning or inheriting money and, as I recall, my only winnings - apart from those recorded in "The Rollright Stones" was a double jackpot on the fruit machine (one armed bandit) at the age of ten. Even then it was my aunt who actually put the money in the machine as I was too young to go into the bar!

To put it another way "Saturday's Child works hard for a living."

Not only did I not win the money but for the next twelve months a magazine dropped through the door and I felt I ought to read the damned thing as I had paid for it!

I think, I hope, I pray I have learned these lessons after the last incident which occurred in January 1989.

When the document came through the door I inspected it very carefully having been caught out so many times before. I had been chosen to receive a prize and whilst the company did not know which particular prize I had been awarded they assured me it would be one of the following:

A Fiat Panda Car
£300 in cash
A video recorder
A microwave oven
6 nights in Florida

All I had to do was to telephone the company, make an appointment to visit their premises and collect my prize.

When I telephoned I was immediately struck by the downmarket manner of the telephonist who took my call. Did I realise what this was about, she asked me. I wondered what was coming. You do know it's timesharing, don't you? I paused for a minute but still could not see a catch in anything she had said and she had assured me, as did the brochure, that there was no obligation to buy anything.

So I made the appointment and agreed to spend a couple of hours listening to a presentation. Even the lowest value prize, which I assumed to be a microwave oven valued at over £100 was worth having for two hours attendance - or so I thought. A better question might have been whether I really needed a microwave oven. Or did I want to subscribe to the Reader's Digest.

The Law of Business Balance

The date was set for a Friday afternoon in January and I drove into the centre of a murky, rainswept Birmingham. For twenty minutes I cruised round the packed streets looking for a parking space but none appeared. Was there ever a more obvious signal that I was in the wrong place? Finally I spotted a space, parked the car and walked what seemed like miles across the drenched grey labyrinth of inner city Birmingham.

I was greeted by a receptionist - as down market as the voice on the end of the telephone - and ushered into a room where perhaps a hundred other people were seated round small tables in groups of two or three. Tea or coffee was offered but the ambience was very definitely utilitarian, a sort of staff canteen displaced from factory to high rise office block. An amiable young man in a purple pullover was assigned to me and proceeded to execute the standard sales procedure.

Having recently been on a Sales Training Course myself I could detect the script he had learned, the first part of which was to find a topic in which the customer was interested so that a rapport could be established. The problem was that I was not very interested in participating in this

47

process. I was there for my gift - my something for nothing - and saw the rest of the afternoon as a rather tiresome charade. I certainly had no intention of buying a timeshare apartment.

In fairness to the salesman - I'm afraid I can't even remember his name now - he was not at all flustered; not even when he asked me where were the three places I would most like to have a holiday. My answer was New Zealand, Colorado and the Republic of Bhutan - true at the time. If he thought I was trying to be clever he didn't show it but found me the pages in the catalogue where I could buy Time-share in Colorado and New Zealand, apologising for the fact that they didn't have anywhere in the Republic of Bhutan. I am not sure that I would have been as tactful in his position with a customer like me and we even established that he was a Sagittarian, not usually noted for tactfulness.

We went through the whole works, the sales talk, the video, the follow up and finally asking me to sign on the dotted line. When I wouldn't sign they brought in the heavies to discount the price and I recognised all the hard sell techniques which I had learned and refused to use.

We went through the whole works, the sales talk, the video, the follow up and finally asking me to sign on the dotted line. When I wouldn't sign they bought in the heavies to discount the price and I recognised all the hard sell techniques which I had learned and refused to use.

After I managed to make my refusal definite enough for them to give me up as a lost cause I was ushered - herded or discarded might be more appropriate words - into the reception area. Five minutes later I was called outside by one of the down market receptionists who delivered a speech straight at me informing me as she handed me an envelope that I was receiving a voucher which would provide me with free accommodation for six nights in Florida. She also guided me quite firmly towards the door before I could make any reply.

Outside the rain and mist had cleared but the darkness had fallen. In a semi-daze I looked up at the sky as though to find a direction for my thanks - I had finally won something, Fate had smiled on me at last, the prominent Saturn in my chart had been subdued.

If you are one of the many people who have been through a similar experience you will both guess what is coming and wonder how I could have fallen for it - indeed I ask myself the same question. As I emptied the envelope I saw that the voucher was certainly for six nights in Florida *and* was valid for all the family *but* when completing the voucher to book the holiday the instruction was to enclose a non-refundable deposit of £150.

Still in a state of semi-euphoria I could not quite understand the purpose of this request for funds but a closer inspection revealed that this would enable the company to make flight reservations. What!! Accommodation but no flight? The brochure had, indeed, promised accommodation but had said nothing about the flight. As a graduate in English I could not fault their use of language but as a human being I could feel a lot of anger at the callous way in which people were being misled.

Except I didn't feel angry this time because I knew that such a feeling would be simply a projection of the anger with myself for believing that I could beat the common law of business balance.

There are enough examples in the world of arts - from "The Merchant of Venice" to "Indiana Jones and the Last Crusade" (although I did not see that film until some months later) - that all that glitters is not gold; I had tried to get something for nothing. I had assumed that the very least I could get was a microwave oven worth £100 whereas what I actually got was worth far less. It was, in fact, totally useless unless I chose to buy the air fares and if I wanted to go to Florida I could probably arrange a better deal independently from the bookings which this company had made.

A couple of minor half baked schemes have been put to me since that time which I have had little difficulty in refusing so maybe, at long last, Ruskin has finally got his message across to me.

Perhaps I should have taken more notice of the fact that I couldn't find anywhere to park the car.

CHAPTER 10

DEBBIE'S MORTGAGE

It was a sunny Monday morning in early May when Debbie first called. She had been trying to arrange a mortgage, felt suspicious of the broker with whom she was dealing and had been given my name by a friend of hers who had recently taken part in a course which I had run.

I can often get a good idea from the first sound of someone's voice on the telephone of the level of compatibility we might have and, in this case, I sensed a strong connection with Debbie. What could I do to help, I asked.

It was quite simple, she said, she had recently started her practice as an acupuncturist, had no capital, no accounts, no husband, a daughter of nearly two and wanted to borrow £60,000 to buy a house in Leamington Spa. For good measure she had to leave the flat she was renting on 30th. June. What could be more straightforward?

By all the principles of financial consultancy this was not a case to touch with a six foot bargepole. Even in the financial climate of Spring 1989 with a slump in house prices and Building Societies offering everything from free legal fees to pocket calculators in order to persuade people to borrow money Debbie was not a good risk. However, Debbie had spent time at Findhorn and was, therefore, in tune with a way of life that is not always familiar to clients who want such apparently mundane things as a mortgage.

The Findhorn Community was founded in November 1962 by Peter and Eileen Caddy and Dorothy McLean. There is considerable literature documenting this - a good account may be found in "The Magic of Findhorn" by Paul Hawken - but it may be worth recording some of the more salient points here.

Peter and Eileen had been brought together some years previously, both making considerable sacrifices - Eileen left her husband and five children - in order to carry out the work which they believed was their purpose in life. For some years they ran the Cluny Hill Hotel near Forres in the North East of Scotland, reviving an ailing establishment by creating a loving atmosphere rather than the more traditional "hire and fire" methods. They were subsequently moved to

50

another hotel in the Trossachs area of Scotland, later dismissed without explanation and found themselves back in the Findhorn area with nothing but a caravan for the three of them and the Caddy's three children.

Eileen gained access to her Inner Voice and was told to "Be still and know that all is very, very well." Guidance continued to come through Eileen and was acted on by Peter. They camped on the caravan site near Findhorn Bay and followed instructions to "plant a garden."

Legends (and witnessed accounts) abound of the eight foot high delphiniums and forty pound cabbages which grew on the most barren sandy soil for miles around as though by magic. Dorothy McLean was able to contact the Devas - or Spirits - of the individual plants who communicated their needs in terms of nourishment and hence the giant specimens which resulted. The Devas also had much to say about the mess into which Man had got himself and the Planet and suggested that this might be remedied by closer observation of the Nature Kingdoms.

The outsize crops eventually stopped, their purpose having been served once international attention had been drawn to the essentially spiritual nature of what was happening on the shores of the Moray Firth.

The community grew to as many as three hundred, although these days it has reduced to nearer two hundred as people have moved out to start independent businesses. Many courses are run each year from Conscious Cooking to Massage to Meditation and international conferences have been hosted dealing with Education, Environment and Economics.

Essential to the growth of the community has been a commitment to live in the faith that whatever was necessary to its unfoldment would materialise at the appropriate time. According to these "Laws of Manifestation" you have only to ask once for what is required, to be specific in the nature of your request and to believe that you have already been granted it for the object to materialise at the appropriate time - which will be the correct time according to a universal plan; this may not be the same time as you (or your ego) thought it would be!

Once received, thanks must be given for the object. This, of course, can apply as much to a Porsche as a kitchen table and I can think of no clearer example of the power of the choice of using things for good or evil. As I said at the start of this book - it's OK knowing these things but be careful what you pray for! A re-reading of some children's fairy stories and myths may be illuminating.

It is important to realise that this ability is not confined to a special few but is the privilege of everyone if they dare believe it. To live humbly with such power is, indeed, magical.

I cruised into the office of the life assurance company which I represented and checked in my files to find a source who would lend 100% of the purchase price. No problem, I found six or seven but, of course, if they were taking such a risk they wanted a set of accounts. Not possible, I said, the client has only just set up her business. Tough, they said.

I discussed the case with one of my fellow consultants. Not a hope, he said, wouldn't bother with women clients, want the world and nothing in return. You'll never do it. That, of course was all I needed. He also gave me the telephone number of a firm of lending brokers situated down in the South-East corner of England. I 'phoned them - you want money, they said, - no accounts, no problem, not 100%, though, can do you 95%.

And so it went on. I got back to Debbie and told her of the problems I was having, but was loathe to give it up. By this time - a few days after her first call - she was having cold feet about moving anyway and was wondering whether to rent another flat. She 'phoned again the following week and said she had found *THE* house. It was £58,000 but she had offered £56,000. Would I please re-activate my search for a mortgage.

I found another list of possible lenders, 'phoned six of them without success but one of them referred me to an Irish bank. This brought me great hope as I had done a lot of business in Dublin, had a strong affection for the place and was about to re-visit it for the first time in five years.

Yes, said Eamonn, what did my client do for a living. Acupuncturist, I said. Was that medical, he asked. They did special deals for medics, 100% mortgage with no accounts, fine, he said. Just send in the projected income from her accountants. Acupuncturist, I said, ancient medicine, Chinese, very good, try it sometime if you don't mind the needles.

I got back to Debbie who also felt good about the lending source being Irish but said her offer of £56,000 had been rejected. We decided she should try again - a lower offer but a promise to complete by 30 June - because she now had a mortgage available.

The new offer of £52,000 was accepted and Debbie, delighted, 'phoned me back to tell me.

Three days later I got a letter from the Irish Bank saying that they didn't class acupuncturists as medics and would only lend 85% of the purchase price.

I was due to meet Debbie that afternoon for the first time (all our previous conversations having been by telephone) in order to complete application forms for a mortgage which we couldn't get and telephoned to cancel the appointment. Debbie, however, was not at home, and, thinking this might be a sort of cosmic signal, I decided I should make the visit anyway.

I was right. Debbie was unmoved by the change in terms and we agreed that we would arrange for the mortgage through our South East England brokers who had agreed they could get 95% of the purchase price on a mortgage. We pondered over the fact that we had both felt so positive about an Irish lender and came to the conclusion that this had served to get us out of a loop. Without the real prospect of a mortgage Debbie would not have made an offer for £52,000 and got it accepted. I have subsequently seen this same mechanism at work in other cases.

We had moved from wanting £60,000 (3.5 times projected annual income and the highest multiple on which most institutions will lend money) for 100% of the purchase price to wanting £49,400 (2.85 times projected annual income, a multiple with which most institutions would be comfortable) for 95% of the purchase price. What was important was that Debbie had a clear vision of herself actually living in the house and of Ayla, her daughter, playing in it. Vision and reality were beginning to merge.

That still left us with a shortfall of £2,600. Rich relations, I suggested? Possible, she said, the only ones who had money were the ones who disapproved of her. Of course, we both said! But she had written to them, anyway. And they had refused. Friends? She had prepared a letter asking for money by way of gift, equity or loan and gave it to me to read. I suggested some amendments which she agreed. She would mail it in the next day or two. Ask and it shall be granted. I chucked in a fiver to open her appeal fund on the basis that once an idea is given form then it is easier for new energy to be directed to it.

We completed the application forms for the insurance policy and the mortgage.

As we walked to the car Debbie thanked me and said she was so glad that she had found a financial consultant with whom she could talk. I should remember that every time I have a bad day!

A few days later she 'phoned to say she had the offer of an interest free loan of £2,600.

She had mailed the letters and a friend had 'phoned to say that she had meant to offer money earlier in the week. The timing of the offer seemed important. When they had met earlier Debbie had not asked for the money but as soon as she had sent out a signal - by way of letter - the money had flowed in, inevitably from the friend whom she least expected to be of help!

We still had to get the offer of the mortgage sorted out from the ultimate lending source. Then there was an insurance policy to go on risk and solicitors are notoriously slow - even the best of them.

The pressure mounted because of the 30 June deadline. As stated elsewhere, dealing with money always brings up other issues and, for me, because of a strong personal involvement in the case, there was a feeling of responsibility for everything that was happening - an old problem of mine!

Debbie's Mortgage

On one day I managed to generate enormous panic in myself by chasing the mortgage brokers who said the application had not been forwarded to the Building Society although I had been told five days earlier that this had indeed been done. Three hours later I 'phoned them again and was told that the file had been put in the wrong tray and had actually been sent as originally stated. If I had just trusted and left it alone I would not have had any cause for panic!

In my worst moments of horror I could see me being accused of causing homelessness with Debbie and Ayla thrown out of their rented flat and without completion on the house purchase. Oh dear, oh dear. "Incompetent financial adviser in row over mother on park bench" - I could already see the headlines of the South Birmingham Messenger.

After another day of panic trying to get all the arrangements in place before going to Dublin for four days I 'phoned Debbie to apologise and say she would have to do the chasing herself until I came back. I was feeling guilty at deserting my post but Debbie was actually glad of the chance to take part in the process of determining her own future! I recalled an article I had recently written about how consultant and client both taking part in an exercise is a much better solution than both of them expecting the consultant to work miracles. Physician, heal thyself!

In the meantime, Debbie had been to consult a clairvoyant who told her she would not be moving in until August. This gave us both the screaming abdabs as we knew enough not to ignore such advice lightly - and here we were trying to shoehorn the transactions into place by the end of June.

The offers of mortgage and insurance policy came through on 27 June and the solicitor flatly declared that completion could not take place for at least two weeks. In terms of fulfilling the obligation to the vendor, however, we did have a getout since the survey had revealed that some work was required on the damp course and he agreed that this would have to be done before the sale.

By the time that repair work and the legal process had been completed the move was agreed at 28 July so the clairvoyant was a lot closer than the date Debbie had originally specified and to which I had frantically worked.

As I write this chapter in early August I look back on a case which was about much more than a simple matter of arranging a mortgage. Whilst the commission is useful there were many other gifts in the case.

It was important for me, who had left a wife and children, to see a single parent in the jungle of finance and to have the opportunity to provide a safe space in which to deal with the business. The case was also about persisting with apparent difficulties which will be overcome *if the vision is strong enough* and it was about working with enough trust that material needs would be met - although not necessarily from the expected sources!

Finally - and most importantly - it was about two human beings connecting through a process we call business.

I am honoured, Debbie, that you unhesitatingly gave your permission for me to quote the exact facts and figures of the case.

CHAPTER 11

THE EIGHTH HOUSE

I didn't want to write this chapter. I agonised for a long time before deciding to go ahead but, in the end, I knew that it had to be done for it would be too easy to fill the book with fun, magical stories like the Rollright Stones and that would only be showing you, the reader, a part of me and you would be able to lay a charge on me saying "It's all very well for you to say that but you don't have the problems I have etc.etc." And you would be right because I would not have shown you the bits in my life about which I am not very pleased. Maybe even now there are some things which I don't want to include.

It seems to me very important that I should tell this story because in doing so I am making myself vulnerable and believe that that is something which is needed in the world today; for people who are in, or have been in, positions of apparent superiority to admit their imperfections, however painful that may be. When this happens then there is a better chance that the patient, client or reader may be healed but as long as clients and consultants, or patients and doctors, or readers and authors perpetuate the myth of an all powerful expert to take care of someone then the longer the healing is delayed.

Ever since I was old enough to occupy such an office I seem to have been a natural choice to be Treasurer or Custodian of someone else's money. It started with the Social Committee of our Scout Troop when I was about twelve years old. This was a separate entity from the mainstream Scouting activities and "Socials" were held on a Saturday evening. We played table tennis and Board Games, lit nineteen-thirties gas fires in iron cases, drank orange juice and home made cakes, made a lot of noise, harmed no-one and thoroughly enjoyed ourselves.

Somehow I became Treasurer and kept the funds in a small tin box with a lock which could have been broken by a malevolent two year old but we prospered sufficiently to buy more games and replacement table tennis bats whenever someone got too excited and smashed one against the table accidentally on purpose.

The Barefoot Accountant

I knew nothing about astrology then but, years later when I became interested, I discovered in my natal chart that Saturn - the planet of responsibility - was placed in Scorpio - the sign which rules, amongst other things, joint finances, taxes, insurances and legacies - in the eighth house - the area of life which is associated with Scorpio. To put it another way, all the Scorpio qualities are re-inforced. Little wonder, then that I should become Treasurer of organisations, an accountant and an adviser on investment decisions.

Saturn is also the planet which teaches although the lessons may sometimes be painful.

I moved on to my last years at School and found myself again looking after money - not this time as a formal Treasurer but as custodian of a Sixth Form project to produce a school play. Four of us chose the play, cast it, acted in it, produced it, arranged the stage lighting and sound and eventually enlisted a teacher to direct it when we finally acknowledged our limitations.

But we made a profit out of it, some £37 as I recall and I, as Treasurer, was left holding the money which no-one wanted to claim. My three friends, all a year older than I, left for University or College while I stayed at school, still with this £37. No-one wanted to put on a play the following year and we had agreed, rightly or wrongly, that the money should not be lost in the amorphous "School Fund" which was used mainly for buying text books.

Eventually I left school, still with the £37 in my Post Office Account for "safe keeping." My chief desire at the age of eighteen was to learn to play the guitar and so I finally spent the £37 to buy just such an instrument. At the time I tried to justify my action to myself on the grounds that as I was one of the people who had done much to generate the money in the first place there was no reason that I should not benefit from the proceeds.

To this day, I still don't know what we should have done with the money at the time but I'm sure it should not have landed up in my pocket. In later years I tried to justify my use of the money to myself on the grounds that by learning to play the guitar I had sat around many camp fires and enabled people to enjoy a sing-song but somehow my inner self remained unconvinced.

In December 1988 I embarked on a personal clean up - after all, how could I advise people about their money if my own hands were not clean? I duly returned to the school, and as I walked through the front door, ran across the deputy headmaster who had once taught me mathematics.

He had hardly changed in appearance in seventeen years and also recognised me without hesitation; we immediately had a conversation about metaphysics and the way the world was changing which demonstrated how far we had both travelled since he had struggled to impart the Binomial Theorem into my unwilling brain. I confessed my misdemeanor and wrote out a cheque repaying the original sum plus interest and which would be used for a project linking the children of West London with those in either Italy or Russia.

I felt that my conscience was now a little clearer but there was still a rather weightier matter worrying me.

Whilst I knew my hands were clean as far as the various charities with which I had been involved were concerned there had been an unfortunate incident in my early days as an industrial accountant.

The company where I had occupied a job as finance manager was part of a large group struggling with the recession and massive changes in the market and technology. The salaries of the employees were being eroded by inflation and in order to keep up morale a practice had been established in the company some time before I arrived but which it was clear I was expected to support.

The sale proceeds of certain pieces of small machinery which were being scrapped were not entered in the books of account but, the proceeds being in cash, were retained in the safe and were used to provide basic recreational facilities for the staff. It was nothing very grand, a dart board here and a table tennis table there, perhaps a Christmas dinner; arguably items which the company should have provided anyway but which, in the managerial climate of the times, had been prohibited as the one of the ways in which to reduce losses.

Whilst I supposed such practices would not be endorsed by the Institute of Chartered Accountants, of which my predecessor was also a member, the wider benefit of helping people through difficult days allowed me to continue the practice with a clear conscience. Sometimes one can pay too much attention to Rules which were designed for general rather than specific situations.

However, after a few months in the job a piece of machinery was scrapped and, rather than the customary £50 or £100 sales proceeds, the service engineer who had done the deal walked into my office with £700. I have written in the opening chapter of this book of the distress to which many accountants are prone when suddenly faced with large quantities of notes rather than figures on a piece of paper. This was just such an occasion.

Neither of us really knew what to do since we both felt that having such a quantity of money in the rather flimsy safe in my office was not a satisfactory way of protecting the stuff. We were also surprised by the amount received and were caught in a difficult situation - of our own making, of course.

If we suddenly put the money through the books of account then we would be asked why we had not obtained authorisation for disposing of the machinery and to spend that quantity of money on staff facilities would inevitably generate questions about how such items had been funded and why that expenditure did not appear in the books of account. But, to look at it yet another way, was it not better that the machine should be used by someone who could renovate it rather than that it should gather dust in a corner?

Somehow we decided that the best place to hold the money would be my Building Society from where I could distribute discreet quantities at appropriate times.

So that is where it went; and through no malicious

intent to defraud but rather through inertia the money stayed there, trapped by my inability to make a clear explanation to the relevant directors for fear of wrecking a promising career.

Time went on and the incident receded. I left the company and the money stayed with me; we moved house, spent savings on legal fees and wallpaper and, whereas my intentions had been to keep the money separately identifiable so that I could return it when I finally got up enough nerve, somehow it merged and blended and became lost, buried in my subconscious, resurfacing like an unwelcome guest at the celebrations where money was pouring in by way of bonuses to remind me that it needed releasing. It was a frog that needed kissing.

It would have appeared to be a natural sequel to the visit to my old school to have visited my old employer, made a similar confession, written out a cheque and have gone on my way.

Somehow, that didn't feel quite right for reasons I cannot fully explain. It had something, I think, to do with the fact that a substantial part of the company was involved in the manufacture of weapon systems and even though I knew the money was owed to them I was most reluctant to contribute in any way to such work. Even that, though, was not a total explanation until I began to see that I was, perhaps, being a little hard on myself and that maybe I had already paid the debt.

* * * * * * *

Twelve days have passed since I wrote this story. I had planned to continue by suggesting that there is a more universal dimension to debt than a strict repayment of the original creditor. I had reached this conclusion by considering my continuing record of disastrous investments - as recounted in "Business Balance."

It seemed that I was constantly being attracted to situations where I was able to lose money very easily through adopting an attitude of greed. If I had repaid my debts that were properly owing then I would not have had the money to invest in the first place. It is an example of the theory that if you hang on to something that is not rightfully yours then it will be taken from you in one way or another.

However, I wondered if I was being too glib and whether this was in fact an excuse that I was using not to pay back a debt which was still outstanding. I therefore decided to contact the Director of the holding company who was ultimately responsible for the operation in which I worked, my immediate boss having since retired. I had had no contact with this man for a number of years.

I spoke to his secretary and said that I wished to see him on a personal matter and that I had worked for him some time ago, naming the company. She told me how busy he was, just prior to going on holiday - some ten days hence, how he had to spend a day with the Chairman, how his evenings were booked as well but assured me that she would call me to arrange a time for us to meet.

Now he has gone on holiday, I have had no word and doubtless when he returns from holiday there will be a new round of pressing engagements which will prevent him from arranging a meeting with me. I am assuming, therefore, that the meeting was unnecessary, that my attack of guilt was not justified and that I had indeed repaid the debt by virtue of having lost the money elsewhere in the world.

I read more and more frequently of the abuse of other people's money in far greater sums than have ever troubled me but the money, as usual, is only at the surface. When we misuse the money we are holding for someone else we are really betraying their trust which is a very basic human quality; it is easier not to betray that trust if it is placed in us by someone who is obviously vulnerable, a child or an old person, perhaps, but that same quality is required even when a so-called faceless entity such as a large company is involved for a company is nothing other than a collection of human beings. If we accept a position where trust is required then we had better be aware of what that really means.

It was a painful lesson.

CHAPTER 12

TOBY ARNOTT CLIMBS THE TREE

Eight years have passed since Toby Arnott gained
Admittance to the Institute; he's feigned
An interest in such topical affairs
As hit the front page of the Press. He cares
But little for the intimate details
Of legislative change; accounting fails
To stir the secret passion in his soul.
Strategically his medium term goal
Is partnership, a means towards his end
Of shares and gold and property to blend
With money in his swollen bank account.
The ground he's covered we will now recount.
Once qualified and safe with a CV
That showed him one of Britain's brightest three
He carefully studied which professional option
To take within the firm of his adoption.
Interest was high in Corporation Tax -
He knew the firm was trying to relax
The grip the Inland Revenue exerted
On many clients, some of whom deserted
Smoke-grey London for the brighter lands
Where Government would never get its hands
Upon their bonds and property and cash.
He'd seen accountants' faces turn to ash
Upon discovering one omitted phrase
Had ruined an avoidance scheme; he pays
Not just in money but with reputation
And suffers from professional degradation.
Rejecting tax he cast his net to find
Which other sea deserved his gifted mind
And took the more unfashionable course
Of auditing. Some moments of remorse
Were felt on winter evenings, near midnight
Reviewing files, with budgets always tight.
No longer could an auditor be sure
Continuous employment was secure
For, whispers had it, that in certain firms
Some less than A1 chaps had had their terms

63

Cut short, foreshortened, call it what you will -
Unheard of for accountants up until
The law suits and the hard commercial world
The dying nineteen-seventies unfurled.
But Toby's vision broadened for a spell
Upon secondment to Industrial Hell;
The Northern Branch asked for his expertise
(They tried their best to put him at his ease)
In planning jobs for which they'd just been hired.
But Toby's spirit wasn't greatly fired
By foundries or by coal or engineering.
He saw the truth of rumours he'd been hearing
In London of a vast industrial waste.
He never ever thought that he'd be faced
With giving values to extruded brass
Or putting half a workforce out to grass.
The oil and grease and grinding of the mill
Held no appeal in motion or when still.

Toby Arnott Climbs The Tree

Returning to the capital he felt
The ice within his heart begin to melt.
For here were vibrant people - here was life!
His next objective was to find a wife.
Essential for a budding partner to
Display ability to chase and woo
And win a pretty damsel's outstretched hand
Then circl'it with a solid golden band.
Were I a Keats or Donne or Byron I
Would tell the lovers' tale by and by.
However, we're not talking of romance
But Toby Arnott's calculating dance
Upon a ladder reaching to the sky
There to be "Partner - Reed Galbraith and Dye."
So Toby wed Lucinda Whatshername -
Another move in life's enchanting game -
She did him proud, a veritable queen.
Their picture graced the inhouse magazine.
It served, as Toby hoped, to stir the men
Who, by the application of a pen,
Decree the fate of those who stand and wait
For clearance to proceed through Heaven's Gate.
And so, at last, comes Toby's great reward
For, through the years it seems that he has scored
Sufficient merit points to claim a place
Within the partnership; he has a face
Which fits and henceforth he will be addressed
No longer "Mr. Arnott" - like the rest
Who've been conferred as partners - he'll be known
In memos, face to face and on the 'phone
For thirty years until retirement day
By his initials, simply TEA.

CHAPTER 13

OFFICE FURNITURE

Like many other people in the late nineteen-eighties who had opted to leave the so-called security of paid employment and work for themselves the initial investment was one of the first hurdles which I had to jump.

Not, you understand, that I had to buy six lathes, four drills and a factory but even in a Financial Consultancy there are some basic tools which are required.

My computer, bought in early 1988, was clearly going to be important as I needed to prepare training material and wanted to write letters with a respectable typeface to my clients. The car (secondhand Ford Escort) was ready for delivery at the beginning of November, courtesy of some loans from family and financial institutions. All I had to do was invest a couple of months of my time.

To put it another way, payslips would no longer be dropping through the door each month and I planned no chargeable work until January). It was in this climate that I was feeling distinctly uneasy about the apparent necessity of having to buy some basic office furniture. Continuing with the computer on a coffee table and the keyboard on my knees was no longer a viable option.

Having occupied an executive office for some years my collection of personal papers had been housed quite happily at work and it was as much in shock as in dismay that I realised just how many files I possessed, many of which had not been used for months or years but were kept "just in case they came in useful sometime."

Neither did I own a desk, having held resolutely for some years to a rule about not bringing work home in the evenings. The monthly ritual of "sorting out the domestic finance" had been performed on the kitchen table but if I was going to be serious about self-employment then a fresh approach seemed in order.

Well, I'd heard all about the Laws of Manifestation, my need was clear, therefore it would be supplied - wouldn't it? Of course, it's easy to put up a so-called mystical solution entitled "The Laws of Manifestation" from some novelty known as the New Age but to quote the Book of Ecclesiastes

(a rather older source):
"The thing that has been is that which shall be: and that which is done is that which shall be done: and there is no new thing under the sun."
Or, to quote from a different part of the Bible - St. Mark:
"Anything you pray for and ask, believe that you will receive it, and it will be done for you."
So this New Age thinking wasn't quite so revolutionary as it might have seemed at first sight.

Despite having already seen a number of examples of money manifesting - and therefore having every reason to believe it would be there for me when I needed it - I could not recall a time in my life when I had felt quite such a concrete need, not of money in a general sense, but of specific items. At the beginning of October, a month before leaving my job I followed the text book approach and sat down quietly in the spare bedroom which was already in the process of becoming my office. I closed my eyes, breathed deeply and smoothly and summoned up images of office furniture.

Gone were the days when I might have believed that my status could be defined by having a desk in polished rose-wood with leather inlay and a rise-and-fall swivel chair upholstered in maroon leather - not that I had ever had the use of such lavish furniture - for such bulky items would not pass through the hall of the small house in which we were living, never mind stand in the spare bedroom.

What I needed was a basic desk, although I had diffi-culty picturing the exact form of this piece of furniture and, more clearly, a two drawer white metal filing cabinet. My vision was quite definite about this. Filing cabinets can come in many grades of wood whilst metal seems to be a far more utilitarian material; also, I shuddered to think how I could fit all my papers into two drawers but on further reflection this also seemed to be part of an important process for me. Rather than look for a bigger filing cabinet I could pursue a different option and reduce the number of papers in my possession.

This was a vital shift in attitude for me and it is an area where many other people seem to get stuck.

In our haste to carve out a place in the world for our-selves we - particularly in Great Britain - believe we need to buy ourselves a house and once on that road it takes a lot of effort to remember that there is an option at any time not to own a house. But, having got that house we then proceed to fill it with furniture and "consumer durables" concentrating more on whether to buy a new settee for £1,000 than how to put a litre of love and laughter into the air.

Eventually the house is full and so we decide that we need to move to a bigger house; again it is often difficult to see the option that says that we could get rid of some of the items in the house rather than move to another house which in time will be as full as the old one and so weighed down with possessions that it is difficult for the energy flow. We believe that our needs have changed when it is only our desires that have altered.

The "consumer durable" area is a veritable minefield. By this term I refer to cameras and televisions, washing machines and food processors, electric can openers and personal stereos. In many cases there is an underlying illusion put forward that these devices are either for "leisure" or "labour saving" so that we have more time for "leisure" never looking at the possibility that household work might in itself become a pleasurable activity if we chose to make it so rather than accept the conditioning that it is a drudge.

I once spent an entire weekend searching for the lever to unjam the waste disposal unit in the house in which I was living and, unable to find it and getting more and more cross in the process, had to deal with the inconvenience of a sink which would not drain. Monday morning arrived and we still had not unblocked the sink so we had to call the plumber and pay his bill for the position to be rectified. Half an hour after the plumber had left the missing lever suddenly appeared - so much for labour saving devices!

That is not to say that I am against modern technology per se - indeed I am thankful every day for the miracle of the computer on which I am writing this book - but what is vital is to ask ourselves why be believe we need to buy a particular item. Is the need real or imagined?

Having asked for my desk and filing cabinet I proceeded to get on with living for the next few weeks and to make the other preparations for my new work. At times, when still no furniture had arrived I wondered just how effective my chosen method of procurement really was but recalled a recent talk which I had heard where the speaker emphasised that what we need will appear *when we need it* and no earlier. Oh yeah? Sounded like a good caveat to me.

Many people I know claim to gain much from their dreams: it is also part of the pseudospiritual hierarchy into which one can get trapped if not careful. There is a spoken or unspoken assumption that one is in touch with one's unconscious (a spiritual "good thing") to a greater extent if you have good recall of your dreams.

Well, yours truly has to admit that making sense of his own dreams has never been his strong suit. If I dreamed of anything as vivid as lean cows eating fat cows I reckon I also might have a good chance of working out that Egypt was going to suffer famine but my nocturnal journeys seem to be, for the most part, of such extraordinary dullness that my only action is to forget them by the time I wake in the morning.

On odd occasions, though, something does impress itself on me and a dream I had during October 1988 was one of these. Well, dream is rather overstating the case as I woke really with a single fragment - that fragment being an address, 20 Greenend Road, which had etched itself very clearly in my mind and which was three doors away from the house in which we lived.

I suppose this dream was on a Monday or Tuesday and I really did not know quite what to make of it. Was there somebody living at number twenty who would be important to me? Or a warning not to go near there? I carried this around with me for a few days not knowing what to do with it and in the meantime neither a desk nor a filing cabinet came my way.

On the Saturday morning, a week before I was due to leave my job, I had resigned myself to the fact that, clear as I thought my vision had been, the so-called magic had not entered my life and I would have to go and buy a desk and filing cabinet. Whilst I had no desire to have new furniture - nor did I have the means to obtain it - I supposed I would have to hunt around the second hand shops and was ready to pay maybe £50 for a desk and, if I could find one, £20 for a filing cabinet. Well, perhaps, I could find £70 after all.

On the way out of the house to the furniture shop I amost fell over our neighbour in the drive which we shared who was busy loading furniture into the back of his car. We stopped to talk for a few minutes and he told me that he was helping to move everything for his son who had just taken possession of his own flat and was therefore leaving home. I asked whether he had a desk which he didn't want as I needed one. No, he didn't. Ah well, I thought, that would have been too simple.

The house in which we lived was at the mouth of a T-junction as a result of which, when I parked on the road, I could swing the car round in one movement and drive off without delay. That morning, however, I was still pondering on the dream I had had earlier in the week and drove the car slowly towards 20 Greened Road.

I stopped for a moment, still uncertain what to do. I reviewed the possibilities. Should I knock on the door and say "Hello, I had a dream about your house four nights ago!" and see what happened? Even with the self-confidence I was beginning to acquire I had grave doubts about taking such action for fear of either being dragged off to the nuthouse, hauled before the police for causing a Nuisance or simply being thumped on the nose for impertinence.

I waited maybe a minute, surely no more, but the door did not magically open and so, having now driven past the mouth of the junction, I started to manoeuvre the car round, a rather more lengthy and complicated operation than I usually undertook to get to the main road.

Eventually I was in position and just changing gear as I

passed my neighbour who was no longer trying to load furniture into his car but was running towards me excitedly waving his arms to catch my attention.

"We *have* got a desk we don't need," he said, rather out of breath. "I thought my son was taking it with him but he said he doesn't want it, I think he's bought a new one."

Well, now. Something had happened. I was more excited, I think, about the underlying mechanism than the fact that I had actually got a desk. I was unsure whether I was being offered the desk for free but, more I think in a spirit of thanksgiving that miracles were working I offered my neighbour £7 which he accepted.

On any other morning I would have swung the car round without delay and driven off. I shudder to think how frustrated I might have felt if I had returned home having spent £50 on a desk only for my neighbour to have offered me one later in the day. 20 Greenend Road, it seemed, had played its part in delaying me sufficiently for that process to unfold and I never did knock on their door nor they on mine.

The week progressed and on the Thursday afternoon, my penultimate day at work, we were discussing some important matters in the office. By that I mean questions of our purpose here on Earth, the concept of re-incarnation and the use of astrology for making business decisions rather than the usual topics of conversation which had to do with how we might report a smaller loss that week to Group Accounts or whether to re-organise the office furniture in pursuit of greater efficiency.

I related the story of the appearance of the desk as an example of how things seemed to move beyond the rational way in which we had been taught. However, I commented, the filing cabinet had still not turned up.

"Oh," said Joanne, "We've got a filing cabinet in our garden it's only got two drawers and it's a bit rusty but you can have it if you want it."

Sure enough, the following morning, my last day at work, the filing cabinet arrived in Joanne's car and we moved it into mine. Indeed it was a bit rusty and its grey colour reminiscent of many a Black Country office in which I had worked over the past dozen years. I remembered that my vision of the filing cabinet was very clear about whiteness and felt that some physical work was appropriate.

By rubbing it down, clearing away the accumulated rust and putting on a coat of fresh white paint it seemed I would be performing an act of physical transformation, symbolic of what was happening on many levels for me at that time. Do-It-Yourself has never been an area in which I have been very confident but this was something I felt I could manage.

That weekend I bought some paint, sandpaper and brushes and worked happily in the Autumn sunlight; no matter that the paint ran or that a better technical job could have been done by many an apprentice at the local car factory. It was my own song and I enjoyed singing it.

As I settled down to work the following week, having thrown out file after file so that what remained could fit into my cabinet I reflected on the events of the past month.

At one level, I was delighted to have got a desk and filing cabinet for an outlay of £11.36. As a bonus, I had found in the filing cabinet a ruled cash book which was perfect for keeping my accounts, an A-Z of Birmingham and a tray which I placed on top of the cabinet to hold my papers.

At another level, I was deeply happy about the excitement of the journey which had got me to my destination. Other people had had the opportunity to share an adventure and to witness some magic; in doing so the paths of our lives had touched where they might otherwise have continued in parallel.

Is our destination so very important or is it the quality of our journey which is more crucial?

Is reality a dream? Maybe we dream to find reality.

CHAPTER 14

LAKE WINDERMERE

In April 1989 I went to consult an astrologer in the Lake District. Having recently made a conscious decision to reduce the number of miles I drove each month this was an ideal opportunity to use public transport. I researched the times, costs and routes of the buses and trains and eventually decided to take the train from Birmingham to Lake Windermere a distance of some one hundred and seventy miles. From this point, however, the train service ceased and the last twenty miles would have to be covered by a local bus.

Except that I had always loved hitchhiking but had not done so for nearly fifteen years.

I arrived at Windermere and set off from the station along the road into the town, the fresh April day noticeably cooler than when I had left Birmingham. I stuck out my thumb but no-one stopped and after a little while I realised that I did not actually want anyone to stop - so much was I enjoying the walk.

When I was tiring and actually needed a lift I was fortunate enough to get one and my initial frustration that the driver was only going three miles out of the remaining eighteen of my journey was tempered by the fact that he dropped me outside one of my favourite Lake District bookshops where I bought three books which I subsequently found both useful and enjoyable.

I picked up another ride soon afterwards and arrived for my appointment at precisely the time we had agreed - no wonder I had had to wait for lifts, I didn't need them any earlier!

The consultation was both moving and full of fresh insights for me. Not for the first time I found myself contrasting the process of healing through self knowledge (using whatever form) with the apprehension I had often felt in the unfriendly atmosphere of a National Health Service waiting room. Changes, I knew, were coming, but oh, how slow they could sometimes seem.

And then I had to stop myself from teetering over the cliff marked "alternative snobbery" for too often I had seen the superiority of "alternative" practitioners brought into conflict with the "orthodox" practitioners - precisely the sorts of behaviour which "alternative" practitioners professed to cure in others!

Returning to the station at Windermere the following morning threatened to be a little trickier than the outward journey; it is one thing to be late for an appointment when the rest of the day is available; it is a different matter to miss the train and have to wait several hours for another.

As I left the house I was faced with a mile to walk uphill where there were few places that passing cars might stop. Sure enough, none did and as I climbed further the crispness of the previous day began to give way to the more familiar Lakeland rain; at first a fine drizzle and then weightier drops lashing into my face as the wind swirled.

I reached the top of the hill and the road levelled. Cars seemed to be few and far between and I began to have some concern about the time. It was around ten o'clock and the train left at half past eleven. The car journey would take twenty-five minutes but to walk would take six hours - well there was a bus around mid-day. . .

The cars that passed were mostly new ones, brightly painted, many with only a driver and no passengers. I saw the reflection of my past, an executive in the warmth and dry. And yet I felt no resentment for I had my freedom - even with the wetness in my hair and on my cheeks and I was holding fast to the Trust that I had placed in getting to the station on time. Car after car passed - every time I held my thumb out and a bright red car approached I knew it would not stop. Not even the lorries - normally a hitchhiker's best friend - wanted to stop this morning.

I knew my lift instantly when it approached. A twenty year old Volvo - the sort that are used as advertisements for the durability of that make of car. It was driven by a young electrician and I clambered into the front seat; again I felt I was travelling back in time, so basic was the interior of the car compared with today's models. The seats were leather, the only dial on the dashboard was a simple speedometer and the radio was a transistor bolted on to the dashboard. It may have had a cassette facility - I can't recall for certain - but if it did it was not of the quality to which most people are now accustomed. The shape of the car, also, was very strange; it felt as though I were sitting in an egg rather than the flattened, wedge shaped vehicles of the nineteen-eighties. eighties.

I had about ten miles in this car, the electrician totally unconcerned about my wetness or why I was hitching. He dropped me in the pouring rain just outside Grasmere and I scrambled to my feet thinking I might get a lift from the lorry we had passed a mile up the road. He passed by but the car behind him stopped, a beaten up old Vauxhall with two holidaymakers who had crossed the border from Scotland.

I had waited twenty seconds for my next lift, again in a very downmarket vehicle.

This lift took me only four miles, into Ambleside where I had bought books the previous day and I was left with five miles to do in twenty minutes. I walked through the main street holding out my hand without a lot of hope as getting lifts in the middle of traffic is not the easiest task.

If I had thought that my last two vehicles were tatty then the piece de resistance was yet to come - a decaying old rust trap of a Bedford Van and a driver who looked as though he had slept under Waterloo Bridge for the last six nights.

But he had stopped: this man and the other two owners of beaten up old vehicles were happy to share what they had with me whilst the drivers of luxury cars passed by pretending not to notice.

I got into the van, a little nervously I must admit for he had a vociferous Alsation chained in the back. Somehow we got talking about work and I said that I worked with money.

"That's good," he said "you can tell me what to do with these," and he produced a wad of official looking papers which he had received in connection with some Unit Trusts he held.

Many of my prejudices were still firmly in place. Firstly, I was not desperately interested in wading through the thick prose and secondly there was no return in it for me, this was a poor farmer, surely. Maybe he had £500 in these trusts.

"I should hang onto them," I said, rather dismissively, not really bothering to take them very seriously.

A couple of minutes later he was telling me that he was probably planning to sell half of his holding of £25,000.

Too late, I tried to explain how I could help to find a home for his money.

We got to the station on time, I caught the train and, when I was home again, I sent him the brochure as promised. However, I had an uncomfortable feeling that I had probably blown it. Two months later I knew for certain that was the case. Feeling that a telephone call might persuade him we could do some business I asked directory enquiries for his number but it was ex-directory and so I was unable to make contact except by a second letter which I deemed inappropriate. I had "lost" this one but learned another valuable lesson.

The Universe had offered me business on a plate which would have paid for my two day trip to the Lake District many times over but I had been foolish enough to hide my energy behind assumptions, preconceptions and judgements.

Abraham, entertaining angels unawares, let his energy flow rather more freely.

CHAPTER 15

WORKING BY DONATION

In the Autumn of 1988 I struck out for new territory when I announced to a meeting of the Business Network in London that I would be holding a seminar some two months later, the object of which would be to give participants the ability to understand accounts.

The Business Network comprises some two hundred people, perhaps seventy of whom attend a monthly meeting with a guest speaker. The theme of the network, basically, is that there is more to business than simply making a profit; a company will also need to consider the way in which it relates to its employees, customers, suppliers and the environment. Indeed, failure to do so is likely to impede any ideas of making a financial profit which is sustainable in the long term.

My announcement was greeted with some warmth as I made it clear that the subject matter would be treated in a lighter fashion than is usually the case with finance and would be, hopefully, a "user friendly product." Considering that it takes at least three years to obtain any sort of accountancy qualification this may have sounded a little ambitious but I was determined to help those people who wanted to do so make the first step along the road to understanding finance for themselves rather than having to rely on an "expert" to interpret the accounts for them.

Having found suitable premises I had been very uncertain about fixing a rate for the course. On the one hand I was targeting the so-called alternative market where events might only cost £20 or £30 per day whilst the full commercial rate for a course on "Understanding Accounts" could be as much as £150 for a day. Neither did I want to undervalue myself; after much debate I went for a figure of £40 and sent out the leaflets.

Nothing happened.

About three weeks before the seminar was due to take place - and still without any firm enquiries - I decided to cancel it and the following day I telephoned the owner of the premises to tell him of my decision.

It can only have been a day after that when I had an
cnquiry from someone who was most disappointed when I
said that the seminar had been cancelled.   Then there was
another enquiry.   And another, so that if I had gone ahead
I would finally have had about six or seven people which
would have been suitable and the seminar would have been
financially viable.

That was my first lesson; if you are going to do something then commit to it and what you need - in this case
customers - will arrive in its (their) own good time.

Having found that there really were potential customers
in my mailing list I resolved to give the seminar in the Spring
once I had established various other aspects of my business.
I duly booked the hall again and decided, come what may,
that I would be there for the seminar - even if no-one else
was!

Many of the events which I have organised over the
years have been teaching me about the so-called "numbers
game."   Roughly stated, this says that an event is deemed to
be a success or failure according to the number of people
who attend.   In certain cases, the "Live Aid" concert for
example, the presence of a large number of people and the
general feeling of a successful event may well co-incide but
there are many other occasions when they do not.   It is easy
to count numbers; instruments to measure the energy type
and level which is present at an event are not as widely available.

Certainly there have been times when I have felt more
lost and dissatisfied at a gathering with fifty people than at
one where there were only four of us and which, by
numerical analysis would have been deemed a failure.

I arranged two days on which to present this seminar
and three people attended on each of them.   The original
bookings had been for four on the first day and two on the
second day but, due to a train strike, one person could not
get to the venue on the first day and just turned up on the
second "on the off-chance" which produced a much better
balance than would have resulted from the original booking
pattern!

My commitment to being there was tested by the Tube
strike.   I stayed some four miles away from the hall and, on
setting off on the first morning, found that my fears over
lack of trains were confirmed and that I would have to take a
bus.   Or so I thought until I saw the queue at the bus stop
and the snail like pace at which the traffic was crawling.

There was only one thing for it, I would have to walk and strode out along a route which I had walked often in my teenage days.

Ever the optimist, I had thought that I would just be able to arrive at the venue in time but the distance was further than I had remembered and I had forgotten that it was asking too much to keep walking at the same pace at which I had started. Running, and getting too hot that April morning, did not seem condusive to starting the seminar in a composed and relaxed state.

Relying on the principle that what you need will come to you - and feeling a strong commitment to getting to the seminar on time and in good shape - I put out my thumb and started hitching. In the two miles I had walked not one bus had passed me, so slow had been the traffic, but now the jam was thinning and the cars were moving more freely. I knew that the bus I would have caught, had I waited instead of walking, was still a long way behind me.

It could have taken no more than a minute for a car to stop for me - not just any car but an air-conditioned Mercedes whose driver had been on the road for two hours making a journey that would normally take twenty minutes.

I made a mental note to get rid of judgements I had formed two weeks earlier in the Lake District about drivers of expensive cars not stopping for hitchhikers!

I sat in the lavishly upholstered front seat and listened to tapes of Middle Eastern music. We talked a little but the ride was not a long one, perhaps ten minutes at the most, although it would have taken another half an hour or more to walk.

The Barefoot Accountant

We arrived at the hall at exactly nine o'clock, the Jewish, Barefoot Accountant clothed in a leisure suit with briefcase in hand chauffered by an Arab in a limousine.

I was ready for whoever else should make it through the traffic.

On both days we spent time looking at the issues that money produces for us as well as the nuts and bolts of a set of accounts and we laughed a lot.

Having wondered whether my fee of £40 per particpant had been appropriate when I had tried to organise the seminar six months earlier I decided this time to conduct an experiment and see how it felt to work by donation.

The system is as simple as it sounds; instead of charging a fixed fee, participants are at liberty to give as much or as little as they want. I had attended one workshop under this system and felt it was something I should experience from a different angle.

It raised important issues for me and I felt happy with the way I dealt with them. The first point of interest is that the fees from the six participants totalled £235, an average of almost exactly the £40 I had originally planned to charge. However, there was a wide range in the six individual amounts and I was glad that I was able to feel as good about those who gave less as those who gave more.

It felt to me as though it had been necessary for all six of them to be there and that without each one of them something would have been lacking. Who is to say whether those who gave more would have done so if those who gave less had not attended; the whole energy of the days would have been different and it is certain that I learned much from both workshops. Amongst other things I began to learn to accept what people have to give - which may not always be in the form of hard cash!

Some of the participants wanted to pay at a later date, perhaps to consider the amount more carefully or maybe because they were waiting for some cash to come in first but whatever the reason it was a wonderful opportunity to create an atmosphere of trust by saying that they should pay when and how much they wanted. I also enjoyed having bits of money come in over the next couple of weeks and to raise individual invoices for each person. The whole process was another example of what business can be like - a far cry from the agitated shrieks of credit controllers in Black Country foundries.

That time seems to be having important consequences

for me; it was an occasion when I made a definite statement about being available to provide a safe space in which to learn about money - even if there were only a few people at those two seminars. Yet, as a result of that meeting I was contacted some weeks later by a friend of one of the participants and we were able to do some business which was not just profitable financially but was based on a relationship in which we both took responsibility for the work. And just a couple of days ago someone with whom I had not spoken for many months telephoned to say that my leaflet had found its way to her and there is now the possibility of some more work.

More people with whom to meet and share. A vast, continuous process of unfoldment in which it is the mystery of adventure which excites and thrills. Who is to know what Grand Opera may eventually be written from the tune that is hummed in the woods one winter's afternoon. To sing your own song is what is important, and if there is no-one in the neighbourhood to hear it matters not, for the more strongly that song is sung the further distance will people travel who wish to resonate with its magical pattern of notes.

Sing your song for all it is worth; nobody else can make the same music.

CHAPTER 16

THE PRACTICAL BIT

It's all very well to read the book or to sit in a seminar and listen to the speaker but, however funny or enjoyable the text or the speech, there is no substitute for experiencing something yourself rather than secondhand.

So, here are a few exercises which might be of interest in looking at money and pointing to some of the other issues which are raised when we are dealing with money. I suggest you take these one or two at a time rather than trying to work through all of them at once.

1. Find a favourite tape of music which relaxes you. If you have any of the New Age type music then this is ideal, if not then try something from the eighteenth-century composers - Bach or Vivaldi or Albinoni for example - I particularly like Pachelbel's Canon in D for this type of exercise.

Allocate yourself some time without interruption, refusing to answer telephones or doorbells (switch on the answering machine if you have one, if not then trust that whoever called will call again if they need to speak to you).

Find yourself a comfortable position and listen to the music with your eyes closed. Relax each part of your body, starting with your feet and gradually working up to your head. Don't hurry this part of the exercise. Empty your mind and let it become like a blank film ready to receive impressions.

Call for a time in your memory when you received money and felt really pleased about it. We don't always receive money gratefully, an overdue debt may not be received with the same feeling as an unexpected present.

Let your mind go blank again.

Now call for a time when you gave money and felt really good about it. Again, there are many different feelings associated with the way in which we pay money. Did that cheque you paid to the taxman feel the same as the money you used to buy a present for your best friend?

In each case, look beyond the financial transaction which took place to the *feeling* that was associated with it. If you are now happy with that feeling find a symbol associated with it which will help you to recall this feeling when you deal with money in the future.

You remembered how good it felt to give and receive money, would you have it any other way?

2. This is an exercise for two people.

Look into your partner's eyes and say the words "I trust you" ten times, slowly. Mean it. When you have both spoken these words, express your feelings to one another about what the exercise meant to you.

3. In a group of three people firstly choose yourself the identities 'A', 'B' and 'C'. Imagine that you are siblings whose father died years ago and whose mother died recently.

You have just received news that your mother's estate is to be distributed to the three of you in the proportions one half (to 'A'), one third (to 'B') and one sixth (to 'C'). The total value of the estate is £30,000. What do you feel about the situation in relation to your parents, your siblings and the money?

4. Try exercise 3 again - but this time the value of the estate is £300,000. Although this might be considered by some people to be a large sum, it is actually a long way below the value you expected the estate to yield.

5. As a final variant on exercise 3 change the situation so that the money is received by the three siblings from an aunt who was generally disliked and who was not believed to be wealthy but who left her estate to the children of her very dear brother (your father). The estate is worth £1,000,000 due to the unexpected discovery of a valuable painting in her attic.

6. Another exercise for two people.

One of you is a graduate trainee with a large corporation and the other is the boss. The latest round of pay increases has just been announced and the trainee considers these to be totally inadequate (perhaps he has a wife and children or ageing mother to support - write your own script). Explain to your boss why the figure should be revised. The boss can elect how to deal with this - it may be a refusal to talk or an explanation that the company is in difficult times or whatever - again, write your own script.

7. Write down how you would spend £10,000.

8. Write down how you would spend £100,000.

9. Write down what you would plan to do for the next twelve months assuming that unlimited finance is available.

10. This one requires two people again.

You are business partners and have received demands

for a pay increase from your workforce of 15% which you have consistently refused since you believe this would threaten the long term viability of the business. Partner 'A' goes away on holiday and returns to find that partner 'B' has agreed to award the 15% and has signed an agreement with the workforce to that effect. Role play the discussion between the two partners that follows this disclosure.

11. You are a research scientist who has been asked to present a paper in Sydney, Australia at a conference which could give you the major breakthrough by way of international recognition and a considerable upturn in your financial position.

You have little money and have therefore arranged a special deal flight at a very low rate - certainly the ticket can not be transferred to another flight. On arriving at Heathrow Airport in London you find that you have left your passport at home in Edinburgh and the flight is due to take off in three hours. What do you do? I don't know you well enough to say whether you have enough money to purchase another ticket - you'll have to write your own script!

12. Now that you have managed to identify your dreams in exercises 7, 8 and 9, how are you going to make them come true?

13. Imagine you are an investment adviser and have suggested that your client invests in a particular company which you think is likely to perform really well, in fact, as you said to the client, you would stake your reputation on it. The client has accordingly instructed you to invest £30,000.

Three months later there is a public announcement that the company in which you invested for your client has gone bankrupt with little hope of any of the money being recovered. Either decide how you are going to handle the next conversation with your client or, if you have a partner available, then actually role play the conversation.

14. Try exercise 13 again but this time the client is either a close friend or relative rather than a previously unknown client.

15. Try exercise 13 again - this time it's your money!

16. Find some more of that music you were using in the first exercise and get yourself into that relaxed state again.

Maybe you would like someone to guide you through the following exercise by reading it to you. The entire process should take around fifteen minutes.

Concentrate on your breathing . . . . . breathing in

through the nose and filling your stomach first . . . . then your chest . . . . . when you have breathed in as far as you can, just rest awhile . . . . . . enjoying the stillness . . . . and slowly let the air out again . . . . . . open your lips slightly as you breathe out . . . . . resting again when you have finished . . . . . . just waiting for the air to return to your body.

Repeat this process, perhaps ten or twenty times, until you feel comfortable that it is taking place entirely smoothly . . . . . . without force.

Now shift your focus . . . . see yourself standing on the edge of an ocean . . . . . . your breath as the water flowing in and out . . . . . . as regular as the tide. Notice that the process continues completely of its own accord . . . . no strain or effort is required.

Repeat that for another ten or twenty times . . . . whatever is comfortable.

Gradually . . . . . . see the waters of the ocean turning in colour from blue or green to gold . . . . . to liquid money . . . . if the gold does not represent money to you then you can change it into something that has monetary value . . . . you can be standing on the beach at the edge of an ocean of dollar bills or £50 notes but . . . . . essentially . . . . . notice that the movement of the ocean continues . . . . whether it is gold . . . . . or money . . . . . . or water . . . . or your breath.

The tide flows in . . . . . . and it flows out again. When it flows out . . . . trust that it will return. Your breath will return . . . . . . when your body is ready . . . . . . the tide will come in . . . . when the sands are dry . . . . money will flow in . . . . to meet your needs . . . . . . just trust.

Slowly . . . . slowly . . . . . . come back from the sea of gold . . . . . . to the ocean of water . . . . to your breath . . . . . . and open your eyes.

Smile.

CHAPTER 17

LIFE ASSURANCE

One of the areas of work which I undertook when leaving employment was to become a salesman for a life assurance company.

If anyone had told me five years or even one year previously that I would be asking people to sign on the dotted line for something as apparently nebulous as life assurance I would have laughed them out of court. However, I was drawn to the industry by a friend who has the highest degree of ethical standards and, I thought, if he is involved then it can't be all bad.

The financial services industry, like any other, is made up of individual people rather than having its own identity as a big bad monster and it is the behaviour of the individual which is important, even in the most adverse of circumstances. In such ways is the world capable of change for better or worse.

Also, I recognised that such work would provide me with an excellent vehicle for learning some important lessons - not the least important of which was how to value myself a little more. There is a vital difference between the salesman asking for business because he sees this as the means to provide his next meal and the salesman who, when he has just failed to make a sale regards it as the client's problem rather than his own that a common sense offer has been refused!

The work fits in very well with my other interests for the mechanism is one of self-employment rather than employment which means that I am free to work as much or as little as I want, have the advantage of being able to access an office environment and the opportunity to find clients with whom I can establish a good long-term relationship.

It is also about rather more than simply selling life assurance policies. The work can be approached from a holistic viewpoint by which I mean that there are a number of distinct features in the process of the sale.

The salesman assesses the client's needs, recommends the appropriate policy (which can be one of a number of different types of insurance policy, a pension, a mortgage or a means of investing a lump sum) and decides *with* the client which underlying funds should house the money. Most companies operate a range of funds where the fund managers use the policyholders' money to buy shares in different types of business ranging in risk from the British Government to Smaller Japanese Companies. In my view it is important - and infinitely more satisfying in my experience - when the client takes responsibility *with* the salesman for the investment decision.

Once the sale is made then a foundation for the ongoing relationship is made and the opportunity exists for future business transactions to occur - maybe even crossing generations. A holistic approach to money is as far removed from the "foot in the door" salesman as the holistic healer or doctor - with time to devote to the patient in an environment of calm and loving support - is from the crowded surgery of a National Health Service General Practitioner on a Monday morning.

Having come from an industrial job where pensions were always at the bottom of my in-tray and where I had seen many pension arrangements - including my own - messed up I felt an instant readiness to understand this topic in more detail with the object of concentrating on selling pensions almost to the exclusion of everything else. Hardly the all-round approach which I have just been recommending.

In part this was to do with my still unresolved approach to the concept of life assurance. Some of the New Age thinking which I had heard was very dismissive not just of insurance but also of pensions. Indeed, such an approach is frequently defended as being entirely consistent with the Laws of Manifestation. A further stage in this type of argument says that if the money does not manifest then it was not needed and one of the lessons which the individual needs to learn was how to cope with loss or poverty. I even know of a case where a business was destroyed by fire and the owner had no more intention of insuring it when it was rebuilt than he did before it was destroyed.

Well, I accept that may be a stage on the spiritual path for some people but it is not mine and such attitudes have a dangerous scent of dogma for me, reminiscent of some of the more fundamentalist positions in various religions with which I feel distinctly uncomfortable. If such a position is valid, however, then I would liken the concept of life assurance or pension planning to providing a pair of water wings for a child before they are confident enough to swim on their own.

It is perhaps worth mentioning, however, that there have been some instances where I have sold insurance policies to clients - New Agers included - who needed them because the other financial institutions with whom they were arranging loans do not live entirely in accordance with the Laws of Manifestation and wanted security for the money which was being advanced. We do not live in an ideal world and maybe it is important that we never will.

What *was* important in those cases for me was that the underlying intentions of my clients were ones with which I was sympathetic. That is not so much a question of judgement on other people's actions as a statement that similar energies attract each other and whenever I fail to make a sale it is almost invariably because there has been a mismatch in the relationship rather than any intrinsic deficiency in myself, the prospective client or the product.

That is my present position on the question of life assurance but when I undertook my initial training I was not

Life Assurance

entirely convinced about the need for insurance products.

As part of the training in the course we were asked to write a review of the programme each day and I wrote the following after returning home for the middle weekend of the two week courses:

"To round off the week we were shown a film called "The Widow's Story" which was, in my view, an appallingly crude piece of emotional blackmail. As Joe [one of our trainers] rightly said, this is not a film to be shown to clients in a one to one situation. Frankly, I would never dream of showing it to anybody!

It represented all that I most dislike about the traditional face of the insurance industry, presenting a one sided picture of desolation and attempting to manipulate the emotions in order to sell through fear. Life just is not like that. In practice, the widow is likely to have received far more emotional support than was shown in the film from friends, relations and the like. As for financial support, the cynicism which had been with me from the start of the week over life protection was hardly eradicated by such an unsubtle piece of cinematography. Far from convincing me of the need for life assurance I was feeling quite outraged towards the people who could manufacture such a blunt instrument. I was rather more persuaded by Joe's real life experiences.

And so we came to the end of the week. I breezed across to the hotel, got in the car, turned the ignition key and was met by a deafening silence. This was a rediscovery. In my late teens when I ran a succession of clapped out pieces of ironmongery such an event was almost part of daily life but for the last few years I had been used to an instant response from the engine and a trouble free motoring life.

I was certainly surprised as I had only bought the car two weeks previously and, although the car was secondhand, the battery could be no more than eighteen months old which, in today's terms, was no reason for it to fail, even though I had not been in the car since Sunday night.

Mitch and John helped push and Sarah tried with the jump leads but to no avail. What the hell was going on? In such situations I find that asking that question is rather more use than getting agitated.

Some of you will have known from conversations

89

during last week that I have been a little suspicious about insurance policies in general. Although I find the intellectual challenge fascinating there has been a lingering doubt about the actual necessity for life assurance as, in Micawber's words, "something will always turn up."

I had got to the stage where I was (relatively) happy to help someone else buy life assurance but felt no need of it myself - hardly a good position for a salesman - as I have no feeling of imminent death.

I also had no feeling that my car would not start.

Of *course* Sarah and John and Mitch couldn't help. The whole purpose of the incident was that I was forced to use the AA - an insurance type product which I had begrudgingly purchased earlier in the year. The AA arrived pretty quickly and, although the battery was extremely flat, the car started at the second attempt and I was away by noon.

The AA man insisted that I must have left something on but I knew that the sidelights were off as I had checked them immediately the car failed to start. The source of the problem was a mystery but, after a couple of minutes of the journey, I realised the interior light was on and that this must have been the cause of the problem.

However, it took me until the evening to recall that the reason the light had been on was that I had been squirreling the cassettes away into the glove compartment in case they were stolen - trying to protect my property but still unwilling to examine the potential of financial protection through life assurance!

So, I who had been so confidently saying that I felt no premonition of imminent death, was very gently reminded by a benevolent universe not to be so bloody arrogant! On the way home, I resolved that I must actually take out some life cover and, even if I survived the stage when I had dependants I could always arrange my will so that the proceeds went to places and people which I felt were appropriate.

The moral of this little story seemed to come back to a Biblical text I had stumbled across some months ago from chapter 6 of Luke, verses 41-42:

"How can you say to your brother, 'Brother let me take out the speck that is in your eye,' when you yourself do not see the log that is in your own eye? You hypocrite, first take the log out of your own eye, and then you will see clearly to take out the speck that is in your brother's eye."

How, indeed, could I presume to give financial advice when my own house was so badly out of order!

I shall return to the second week of the course, convinced that, whilst the Universe does provide in abundance, it also requires each and every one of us to take responsibility for our lives which includes making adequate financial provision. My previous reticence to invest in life assurance as I considered it to be a waste of money is replaced by the knowledge that when I die, whether it is next week or in fifty years, the proceeds of that policy will do some good."

I am happy to say that, although it took rather longer than I thought when I wrote that review, I did purchase some life cover. It was yet another area where I had to do something for myself rather than rely on the automatic provisions of my employer which I had done for the previous twelve years.

Life is never still - it is always changing and as I sit correcting the proofs of the book I can say that this work has moved one stage further. I now operate through a firm of brokers as an independent financial adviser. The key word is "adviser", this is very different from "salesman" which further removes me from the "hard sell" techniques with which so many life office salesmen are imbued - or salesmen of any kind come to that.

Who knows where it will all lead?

CHAPTER 18

THE LANGUAGE OF MONEY

The following is a list, in no particular order, of words, phrases and sayings about money. It is by no means exhaustive and you are warmly invited to insert additional entries.

Look after the pennies and the pounds will look after themselves.

Penny wise, pound foolish.

Money makes the world go round.

Money slips through your fingers.

Money is the root (route?) of all evil.

Money can't buy you love.

You can't take it [money] with you.

Where there's muck there's brass.

Money burns a hole in your pocket.

The rich get richer and the poor get poorer.

Rich bitch.

Money isn't everything.

The only thing worse than being old is being old and poor.

All that glitters is not gold.

Money doesn't grow on trees.

A fool and his money are soon parted.

In for a penny in for a pound.

Money talks.

A penny saved is a penny earned.

Money only comes to those who have it.

A fast nickel is better than a slow dime.

Neither a borrower nor a lender be.

Bread.

Dough.

Dosh.

Loadsamoney.

Filthy rich.

Filthy lucre.

Making a pile.

Making a packet.

Diamonds are a girl's best friend.

Feathering his nest.

Well-heeled.
Flush.
Flash.
Coughing up.
Footing the bill.
Shelling out.
Forking out.
A license to print money.
Making money hand over fist.
Debt-ridden.
On tick.
In hock.
Money for jam.
Money for old rope.
Speculate to accumulate.
Nothing ventured nothing gained.
To rip off.
To fleece.
Blood money.
Judas money.
Fool's gold.
Lolly.
Ackers.
Fast buck.
The Midas touch.
Time is money.

When you look through that list it begins to be apparent that the sentiment of these phrases is far more negative than positive and that much of the negativity in the world towards money is embedded in the very language we use to describe it. Expressions such as "filthy rich" and "money is the root of all evil" are among the most obvious examples which have coloured our attitude. Is it any wonder that so many people feel shame about actually having money?

The effect of language is at work everywhere and if we make the short move from money to business we can see the same thing happening.

Businesses (and the sports arena) have, in many cases, become the latter day equivalent of the battlefields in which the men of the family go off to fight. You think I'm kidding? How many times do you hear executives talking about "hitting their target" or success being dependent on developing the "killer instinct."

Salesmen are forever trying to "beat the competition" and as we move into the legal wording to describe corporate structures we find the relationship between companies in the same group defined in terms of parents and subsidiaries. What sorts of emotion is that particular phrase likely to trigger?

Business - certainly in the English culture - has been seen as something which is predominantly a serious matter and certainly not something to be enjoyed. For example, the expense incurred in entertaining customers, prospective customers or suppliers - in fact anyone except employees - is not tax deductable and has not been so since 1965. Admittedly such tax privileges are liable to abuse but nowhere is this more likely than in a country where the idea is deeply embedded in the national psyche that doing business and enjoying yourself are mutually exclusive concepts.

Beauty is in the eye of the beholder and this is as true with money as with relationships. It is a commodity to be used and how we view it says more about us than it does about money itself. Money is a wonderful medium for discovering how we view so many other issues in life.

If we have no money and envy the wealth of others we might find that envy is a problem in our relationships with other people - if we have the courage to face it. If we have an abundance of money but still crave for more then is there also a dissatisfaction with our friendships even though we are being offered the possibility of satisfying friendships the whole time?

There is no goodness or badness about money - only what we attach to it.

My favourite quotation on the subject comes from Tevye, the Jewish peasant milkman, in "Fiddler on the Roof" who looks to his God and says:

"I realise, of course, that it's no shame to be poor - but it's no great honour either!"

CHAPTER 19

EUSTON STATION

I would suggest that we frequently take a very different attitude to spending other people's money than we do to spending our own. I can think of no better example of observing this behaviour than in the area of business travel.

As an aspiring young accountant at the age of twenty-five or twenty-six it used to grate on my nerves that I had to travel by second class train whilst managers in the company were allowed the privilege of travelling first class. Not surprisingly, I modified my view when I was eventually granted such status!

I then thought nothing of charging up £30 for a first class rail ticket from Birmingham to London when I could have got there just as well by second class for £20.

Of course, there are arguments that by travelling first class the passenger is likely to arrive in a more relaxed state and thus be able to function more effectively for his company at the end of the journey. I can't recall ever having heard such an argument being advanced by anyone other than an employee already entitled to travel first class! Far better that we should advance ourselves to the state where we are not affected by our surroundings than blaming the upholstery for our ill-temper.

As is so often the case with money, there is something going on here at a deeper level than the argument itself suggests. In this case it has to do with the notion that one's worth is indicated by the carriage in which you travel rather than the innate value of one's very Being.

So, I had not only travelled first class in trains but had also ordered breakfasts which were larger than my body required and which comprised food of less value than that which I could have eaten at home had I risen a little earlier.

How nourished had I *really* felt by the fried eggs which swam in grease or the tasteless white bread, charred at the edges into a commodity which was passed off as toast on which I spread my marmalade too thickly. My ego had been bloated but my inner reaches had not been fed.

On aeroplanes, too, I had taken the opportunity - as an employee - of travelling Club Class; again the separation was evident but this time in an even more illusory fashion for all that separated us (predominantly) business passengers in the front of the cabin from the common herd in the rear was a rather grimy brown curtain, a complimentary copy of the Financial Times and free booze.

I flew frequently from either Birmingham or Manchester to Dublin in 1983; the stewards took the utmost care to ensure that the curtain was in place and that we were suitably secluded before we were served our plastic tray of plastic meats and cotton wool bread rolls. Liquid accompaniment of large measures of spirit were always available and few people seemed to have realised that there was an option to refuse the drinks, regardless of the effect on the body of a double whisky at seven o'clock in the morning. So much for arriving at a business meeting in a more relaxed state after having travelled Club Class!

Euston Station

The flights to Dublin were only fifty minutes at the most and, on one occasion I recall, this was shortened to about thirty-five minutes due to favourable winds or some other technical factor; I have seldom seen such panic as was on the faces of the hostesses who swept main courses off our laps and promptly deposited desserts so that the entire culinary ritual could be completed within the abbreviated flight time - you've paid for it so you're gonna have it and enjoy it!

Having removed myself from the Corporate Scene in 1988 I started to take a rather different view of business travel and began to increase my vocabulary with words like "Saver", "Awayday," "Period Return" and all the other tricks which had been dreamed up to complicate and bemuse the life of the simple man who just wanted to travel by train from Birmingham to London.

In May of 1989 I had arranged a meeting with an old friend who wanted to discuss the possibility of my doing some training work with his staff. The meeting was set for one o'clock on the 3rd May and I was looking forward to a gentle ride down to Euston Station in London on the train which would be followed by a journey on the Underground to get me to my meeting.

A few days previously I had enquired about the fares and was told that £36 was the standard return fare - first class fares were a non-starter now that I was spending my own money - but that I could get a "Saver" for £13. I elected for the £13 option although I could not return from London using this ticket until 6.40 p.m. Well, even if I *was* hanging around for three or four hours after the meeting I would be saving £23 - or so I thought.

I arrived at New Street Station in Birmingham and asked for a day return.

"Eighteen pounds, please," came the reply.

"No, that can't be right," I protested, "I was told thirteen pounds on the 'phone."

There was a pause, the ticket seller ferreted around in his desk and, without a word, produced a different ticket. I didn't pursue the point but the incident re-inforced a rather deep-rooted suspicion that the Public Service Monopolies will rip you off every and any way they can. My ideals about Trust do not always stay with me in such circumstances.

My prejudices against British Rail abated somewhat with the experience of a trouble free journey and we arrived in London bang on time. I bought a return ticket for the

97

Underground, had a very successful and enjoyable meeting and at three o'clock I was ready to go home.

I had assumed that I would find some way to fill the time until my ticket was valid but my assumption was unjustified and, having concluded my meeting, I felt rather irritated that I had three hours with nothing to do.

I telephoned a friend who lived nearby to suggest that we had tea but all I got was his answering machine - a sure cosmic signal that it was not an appropriate time for us to communicate. Choosing to ignore that signal I nevertheless made the short journey to his house only to find that after greeting me and spending five minutes talking he had to attend to a group of people with whom he was working for the day.

I sat around his house and read books and magazines rather aimlessly until, eventually, it was gone five o'clock and I drifted back towards Euston.

I reached the Underground Station, handed in my ticket and sat waiting on the platform, rather perplexed by the fact that I still had another Underground ticket in my pocket. I was musing on this apparently inexplicable occurrence for some time - it was months since I was last on the Underground and I had worn this suit many times since then - before the truth finally hit me.

On the outward journey from Euston I recalled that at my destination the ticket collector, a jovial West Indian who had been in conversation loudly but appealingly with his colleague, had paid little or no attention to my passage through his domain and I had simply placed my ticket on the counter of his stall.

Indeed I had, but the ticket I had left him was my return ticket to Birmingham - not the Underground ticket which, even now, was being nervously fingered by my increasingly sweaty hand.

What was the phrase I had recently read about Geminis? Something about having the ability to talk their way out of a paper shredding machine? Well, buddy, I thought, here's a test for you.

The part of me that had grown up a little was very pleased with itself, not getting angry but looking at the situation detachedly and welcoming an opportunity for growth.

Some of the other parts were neither detached or calm.

After what seemed like a very long time the Underground train arrived and I was on the way back to Euston.

Where was the problem, I wondered, surely they can issue a new ticket, *I* know I'm not trying to fiddle British Rail, therefore it is fair to assume that *they* will also know that to be the case.

It was a warm evening and the concourse at Euston was crowded.   I had intended to spend the last half an hour before getting on the train buying some rather attractive ties which I had spotted earlier in the day and which I had assured myself I deserved.   Now, it seemed, I had a different money issue with which to deal other than allowing myself a treat.

I cruised up to the ticket counter and, remembering all that I had learned about positive thinking and visualising success, I launched into an explanation of what had happened.   "Look," I said, "I can even show you the stub in my cheque book where I bought the ticket this morning."

There was very little in the way of a helpful response from the other side of the glass, the British Rail official suggesting that I would have to enquire at the Underground office on the far side of the station.   I reflected on the function of the plate glass which was between myself and the official.   At such a time as this it seemed to be simply placing an additional barrier between a stalwart employee, doggedly sticking to procedures and a freelance consultant who was desperate to retrieve his £13.

I found the Underground ticket office where I had been given to understand that dropped tickets were handed in only to be told that this practice had been changed recently and that any stray tickets were destroyed at the end of the day.   If I wanted to reclaim the ticket I had left at Hammersmith then I would have to go back to Hammersmith, hope that the same ticket collector was still on duty and that he would return the ticket to me.

Such a process would probably take an hour and a half which meant that I wouldn't get a train out of London until nearly eight o'clock and wouldn't get back to Birmingham until gone ten o'clock.   To think that I could have been home at half past five if I had bought a different ticket in the morning.

I ruled out the option of two further journeys on the Underground and decided instead to press my case again with the British Rail officials but I may as well have saved my breath.   There seemed to be little human dimension on the other side of the glass and, despite my resolve to remain cool and calm, I could feel myself getting increasingly annoyed.

I demanded to see the Area Manager and was directed to his office.

Behind another pane of glass in the Area Manager's Office was the Area Manager's Representative - a great bull of a man who told me that there was nothing he could do and that it was my responsibility to look after my ticket.

That sort of lecture (alternatively, a statement of the obvious) was all that I needed and I decided to be ASSERTIVE, to voice my anger instead of suppressing it but it didn't quite happen like that and I think I probably sounded rather more angry than I intended (an understatement?).

I had, by this time, become relatively unconcerned about the issue of the £13 but was, I suppose, almost beside myself with rage as other emotions started to surface. Primary amongst these was the feeling of not being trusted and, therefore, being wrongly accused of attempting to fiddle British Rail. Hell, I thought, I'm a Chartered Accountant, how dare you not trust me - although such a qualification is no sure guarantee against the mishandling of someone else's money as the pages of the Financial press will testify each week with an embarrassingly large number of stories of jail sentences for fraud, never mind the skeletons in my own cupboard.

I sat sullenly in the corner of the room, there being no-one else in the office while the Official thumbed through the collection of lost tickets that had been handed in to see if there were any to get me back to Birmingham but, of course, there weren't. I went out of the office, stalked round the station and returned to the Area Manager's Office where there was still nobody else except old Bull Face - presumably he had frightened everyone else away. So much for improving customer relations, I thought.

I was about to launch into another tirade when I caught my breath and recalled an incident that my good friend Danaan had related at a conference I had attended eighteen months earlier.

"Not until midnight."

"That's late."

"Yea, hate the four to midnight shift."

"Why's that?"

"Get all these people coming in with their special deal tickets asking when they can use them and I tell them the answer and then they get cross because they have to wait. Not my fault."

Euston Station

"Have you worked here long, then?"
"Seventeen years." This is said almost proudly, as though he is pleased with his capacity for endurance - whether or not it is enjoyable. I mark him down as Leo with Taurus Rising.
"Enjoy it?"
"Sometimes, not next week, though, because I'm in accounts for two days. Last time I was there we spent the week trying to sort out all the forged cheques that people had written us."
"But when I wrote a cheque this morning for a ticket I had to supply a guarantee card - surely the bank has to honour the cheque."
"That's the theory - but the banks still try and get out of it if they can. Fifty-two forged cheques I think there were."
And I wondered why British Rail refused to trust me.
I don't think I ever learned the Official's name but he knew mine because he gave me a complaint form to fill out for the Area Manager who wrote to me three weeks later to say that I was responsible for my ticket and his Staff had acted properly.
I had recalled someone else's story told at that conference in 1987 and tried it for myself - I had begun to see someone else's reality which had nothing to do with getting back to Birmingham or losing £13; his life had a different script, standing on the other side of the glass with a flock of piranha-like passengers abusing him when he gave them answers they didn't want to hear and taking dud cheques off people on which banks tried to dishonour their commitment. I wondered why he had chosen his particular life.
What was certain, however, and I had now learned it firsthand rather than through someone else's story, was that when we really start to put ourselves in someone else's position instead of screaming with anger at our own inadequacies the possibilities for creating peace in the world are infinite.
The final insult of the day for me arose when I bowed to the inevitable and bought another ticket to get back to Birmingham. The lunacy of the pricing system perplexed me even more for I was offered a single ticket for £19 or a "Saver" for £17 - in other words it was cheaper to buy a ticket for two journeys than one!
I still don't understand that but I suppose someone, somewhere knows what they are doing - maybe.

101

Also, a "Saver" is £4 more expensive when purchased in London than in Birmingham which is supposed to reflect the difference in the cost of living. So Public Services have finally found out about the market place. I wrote out the cheque for £17 with as much love as I could muster, which wasn't a lot to be honest, and asked why I might have been offered an £18 day return ticket in Birmingham first thing in the morning.

That, I was told was what it said - a "Day Return" where I could have returned on any train that day rather than an ordinary ticket (£36) which I could have used at any time in the next. . .

I was getting lost in the complexities of the explanation but what was apparent was that if I had accepted the first ticket of the day for £18 instead of arguing for a further £5 reduction I probably wouldn't have got myself into the mess from which I was now painfully removing myself.

So many lessons in one day were hard to absorb. The overriding one seemed to be that I should see what needed doing (to have a meeting and return to Birmingham in this case) and not worry too much about chiselling at the costs. When you do what you need to do the money takes care of itself. For an outlay of an additional £5 I would have gained three or four hours of relaxation but I would probably have had to learn the lesson somewhere else.

Also, *pay attention* to what you are doing. I once got knocked over by a car because my mind was elsewhere and here I was twenty-four years later still with my head and my body sometimes in different places!

As for authority, well, someone had helpfully suggested a few weeks earlier that when you recognise what Authority really is you don't have any problems with authority.

At least I enjoyed the meeting, had a good lunch, laughed with my friend and agreed that I would do some work for him.

CHAPTER 20

TOBY ARNOTT BRANCHES OUT

Toby Arnott's really made the grade;
He earns, or, more correctly, he is paid,
A salary of fifty thousand pounds
And owns a country house with spacious grounds.
The cheque which comes each month is written by
Chartered Accountants, Reed Galbraith and Dye.
And, at the end of each financial year,
Partnership profits always do appear
To bring his annual remuneration
Beyond a pauper's lifetime expectation.
But Toby's bored - he's bored beyond belief -
By clients who lunch on Beaujolais and beef,
Who ask him in a confidential tone
(In person, never on the telephone)
If they should buy or sell their Stocks and Shares.
Or put their funds in Chippendale chairs.
Such pests he puts upon the stouter backs
Of partners who do personal income tax.
Toby's an audit man, he specialises
In running all the big jobs, he devises
The audit tests for juniors to perform
In order to ensure that clients conform
With every clause of every Act - but wait!
All this has Toby Arnott grown to hate.
His rise within the firm was due in part
To good connections giving him a start,
And part to luck but most to love of money
Which sticks to him like Pooh Bear stuck to honey.
And now, at thirty-five, he's got the cash
Invested where it's safe from any crash,
He needs much more than money he needs power
And craves it every minute of each hour.
So Toby makes a major life decision
Which some might greet with howls of loud derision;
He'll stand for Parliament and put an end
To all the jumped-up workers who pretend
That they can run a business - what a joke!

The Barefoot Accountant

No wonder that the country's going broke.
I'll find, he thinks, a safe seat in the Shires -
The sort of place a Gentleman retires -
Commute to London twice or thrice a week
Where, in the House of Commons, I shall seek
To gain a senior Ministerial post.
At private dinner parties he'd be host
To influential Commoners and Peers
Who'd listen to his commonsense ideas
On Hanging and Trade Union Legislation,
Responding with appropriate elation.
This was the state of Toby Arnott's mind
But when he came to say that he resigned
The partners so much saw his point of view
(This being England, nineteen eighty-two)
They granted five years' absence from the firm
Not thinking he would serve a second term.
Regrettably they only could afford
To pay him half his usual reward;
"But, hopefully, you'll press our cause," they said,
"The days of simple auditing are dead;
Consultantcy's our future, " with a wink
They added and all drunk another drink.

Toby Arnott Branches Out

So Toby tidied up his desk and files
And flattered all the secretaries with smiles
Which "sotto voce," said the time is here
For me to start a brilliant new career.
He planned to leave and never to return
Expecting that in five years he would burn
His mark upon the Parliamentary scene -
Others were sure to follow where he'd been.
Whether he swept in at the next election
Or suffered a constituency rejection
Or entertained political defection
Must presently remain an untold part
Of Toby Arnott's story.   We depart
With Toby from the glass and concrete tower
Where Reed Galbraith and Dye preserve their power.
No doubt the future sometime will reveal
The products and results of Toby's zeal
'Til then, farewell! Our lips and pen we seal.

CHAPTER 21

MONEYFLOW

My training in the business world revolved around the principle that success in business is achieved by good financial control. The phrase "financial control" has two elements to it - when both of these are seen in a wider perspective then we not only start to enjoy our relationship with money but we are likelier to have more of it!

Firstly, there is the concept of trust. Control is deemed to be necessary where trust does not exist and classical accounting encourages a strict segregation of duties on the basis that fraud is less likely to occur where two or more people would have to be in collusion with each other than where one person is responsible for a number of different tasks.

From an operational point of view many companies are prepared to take this risk as they believe the likelihood of fraud is less costly than employing additional staff. Thus, by default, many employees have come to be in a position of far greater trust than classical accounting theory of financial control would recommend.

The other element of financial control has to do with the flow of money into and out of an organisation and the basic principle, which is prevalent in very many businesses, is that collections from customers should be as rapid as possible and payments out are discouraged until the last possible moment. On more than one occasion I have had managers calling in from shops to say that the bailiff has arrived. The result, if this strategy is implemented successfully, is that the company acquires a large pool of cash from which more money can be made through receipt of interest.

It may be that by acquiring this cash the company invests in further projects which energise the economy by creating jobs and additional trade but where the money is held for its own sake then it is a stagnant resource and, I suggest, will generate the desire for collection of yet more cash. Greed begets greed.

The Parable of the Talents in St. Matthew is relevant for consideration here; this concerns the story of the master who gives five talents (a unit of money) to one servant, two talents to another and one talent to a third. On returning from a business trip the master asks for an account of what has happened to his money. The men who held five talents and two talents have invested or traded with it and yield an additional five and two talents to the master, receiving praise. The third man, knowing his master to be harsh and unfair, buried his one talent in the ground and returns it to his master; he is harangued for not using it and for not even banking it to obtain interest. Even without the benefit of a formal theological training I find the story has a clear message - that where money is left to stagnate then negativity will result but where money is kept in circulation then good may come.

As with money so with love. Try reading the parable in St. Matthew and think of a talent as a unit of love - even better, substitute the word "hug" for the word "talent" and see what happens.

Keeping money in circulation is, it seems to me, a more worthwhile occupation than holding it in a storehouse.

The question which then presents itself is how to ensure a healthy circulation of money.

The chapters "Pay As You Earn" and "The Rollright Stones" detail some fairly dramatic incidents in my own career which woke me up to the idea that the best way to bring money into an organisation is to make enough space for it by putting some out first. You cannot, after all, load your kitchen cupboard with the goods from the supermarket until you have consumed what is there in the first place. This, of course, links to the concept in the other branch of financial control - that of trust.

If we trust that enough money is going to come to us to meet our needs then there should be no difficulty in paying money out ahead of time. Note, though, that we put out money for what we *need* and not for what we want or desire. The key here is to focus on the *purpose* of the individual or the organisation; when that is clear then the material require-ments are also clear. It is unlikely that accumulation of infinite quantities of money will be the true purpose of an individual or an organisation. That purpose will have to be decided by the entity in question so good luck in your search!

Once we become aware of the way in which money operates at this level then our approach to the whole game changes. Financial Directors can, for instance, stop harassing their debtors to pay under pressure in thirty days when they will pay with pleasure in forty-five. Even when all the suppliers have been paid promptly it is sometimes possible that the collection period will stick at forty-five days rather than the thirty which is desired.

What may be happening in this example is that management are expressing a desire rather than a need. The ego says that we will all appear in a glowing light to our superiors if we can demonstrate a fast collection time. When we recognise that demonstrating an abundance of love to our Superior is the real game then we play our shots a little differently and the fear of losing our jobs through a so-called inadequate performance vanishes.

To quote from "The Prophet" by Kahlil Gibran

"Work is love made visible.

And if you cannot work with love but only with distaste, it is better that you should leave your work and sit at the gate of the temple and take alms of those who work with joy."

There simply is nc point in grudgingly pressurising customers to pay quickly in order to meet the ego targets set by your organisation.

As I have watched money over the last couple of years I have noticed the truth of a financial model whose rules may be summarised as follows:

1. Money arrives when it is truly needed if the need is expressed and thanks have been given for any previous gifts - these should have been put to the use for which they were requested.

2. When we freely give money - or love, or some other expression of our energy - we will receive it back in at least equal measure.

3. Do not be attached to the source from which the money returns - it will usually not be the person to whom you gave which ensures that an open circulation is maintained.

4. If you give money for reasons other than truly wanting to give it then it will probably not return to you. The £1 coin given in joy to the busker is more likely to return than the £100 cheque to a charity which ensures your name goes on the founders plaque.

Some examples.

In November 1988 when I first started working for myself I spent two months writing training material and knew that I would generate very little income in that time. At the end of the first month I received a substantial tax rebate from the tax year 1986-87 out of the blue. The strange thing was that when I had received a bonus payment in March 1987 I had been taxed at the highest rate due to an oversight on my part in getting my tax code adjusted. So the money I had "lost" eighteen months earlier was needed far more when I actually received it. To continue the story, the payment was too high and I immediately wrote to explain how the miscalculation had been done but not until September 1989 did I receive a revised assessment requesting a partial repayment. I also banked the cheque which was a great help in keeping me solvent in those early days!

In the same month I received my first payment for interpreting astrological charts. I had been doing this for a year on a voluntary basis for friends, not really needing money at the time; as soon as I needed money I attracted people who offered to pay me without me even asking.

* * * * * * *

My friend David who had left a wife and children felt that in order to broaden his perspective on life he would visit an orphanage in India. It seemed important to him that he should see real poverty rather than what is imagined to be poverty in Britain and also to see children without resident fathers who would be a mirror image of his own children.

He expressed this to his new partner, Andrea, who believed it important that she should accompany him. Whilst David had sufficient funds for himself and was willing to pay for Andrea also she somehow was putting out a message that she should fund herself independently. Within forty-eight hours, on a visit to her parents, her father, totally unaware of this conversation, had presented her with a substantial cheque out of a cash sum received on his retirement and asked her to use it for a holiday. Subsequently, their plans changed and the money was used for a different but equally important trip.

* * * * * * *

My friend Linda had left her husband with her daughter Mandy. Whilst she was well supported by many of her family there was some implicit disapproval from her aunt and cousin. When it came to Mandy's birthday the £10 note from the aunt was lost in the post and never arrived whilst a cheque for £5 from the cousin arrived unsigned and had to be returned for signature. It was as though the whole energy of judgement was being manifested through an unwillingness for the money to reach its target.

* * * * * * *

Due to my failure to conform with the rules of money-flow I found that, at one time, I had tax computations outstanding for six fiscal years. If I had informed the Inland Revenue in the first place of the relevant facts and paid the outstanding tax each year I would have saved myself a whole load of hassle but I withheld my energy from the authorities and the labyrinth grew more and more complex. Eventually I commissioned a top firm of chartered accountants to sort out the mess having been informed that my employer would pay the bill as a "perk."

This offer was subsequently rescinded due to a misunderstanding between my various superiors and I finished up paying a bill which was well in excess of the interest I had saved on unpaid tax. I was totally disgusted - mostly with myself - at the whole affair and the final insult came when I received a letter from the accountants reminding me to settle the final bill. I had actually paid the bill and the cheque had been presented to the bank three weeks before the letter from the accountants but there was so little energy in the payment that the money did not even enter their consciousness. This incident also seemed to be part of the way in which I was bound to lose money as a result of the incidents described in "The Eighth House."

* * * * * * *

My friend Peter had helped me through many of my difficulties between 1987 and 1989 and expressed his desire to go to a workshop in Stockholm on conflict resolution. This work is based on the premise that everything and everybody is connected to everything else and that by reducing tension in our individual relationships we help to reduce tension on the planet and bring about peace in the world.

If you've ever wanted to save the world but felt you were powerless and wondered where to start then the answer is in your own backyard with the people in your life. That is just as important as any treaty that Mikhail Gorbachev and Ronald Reagan ever signed.

What better way could I support this work than by offering £100 contribution to Peter to the cost of his trip.

He thanked me and said he would let me know if he wanted to take up my offer. Three weeks later he telephoned to say he was going and could I send the money. I posted the cheque within the hour.

Four days later I was asked to undertake some consultancy work for an existing client; that in itself was a minor miracle as the work I had already done for the client was rather patchy and certainly less than I had originally expected.

One of the problems was that I had agreed to work at a rate with which I was not happy and had therefore put little energy into the project. Having agreed to do the extra work I had a feeling that I should see whether the fee could be increased due to a change in the client's circumstances. Initially I had planned to ask for an increase of £25 or £50 per day at the outside but instead left the question open. The result of my appeal was to receive an increase of £100 per day in the rate which took me to the figure I had requested six months earlier. Needless to say the job was done with new enthusiasm!

Part of the teaching in the conflict resolution workshops which Peter attended is around the Japanese martial art of Aikido. Amongst other things this looks at the concept of the balance between Yin (feminine) energy and Yang (masculine) energy. While we might think initially that Yang is more powerful with its forward and aggressive thrust it is actually when we use Yin, making ourselves vulnerable and receptive, that we are more powerful. By offering my client the chance to name a new rate I had actually gained considerably more than by naming my own figure to which he would no doubt have agreed! It was also an instance where the energy or money which I had given had been returned with interest.

* * * * * * *

A blue moon occurs when the moon is full for the second time whilst the sun is in the same sign of the zodiac. In order for this to happen the first full moon has to be very near the start of the sun's residence in a sign and the blue moon at the end of it. The rarity with which this happens gives rise to the expression "once in a blue moon."

Just such an event occurred in May 1989 and, having planned for some time to hold a party, we decided to mark the blue moon accordingly. The guest list grew inexorably and, having just regained solvency after a few months of

111

spasmodic work, I proceeded round the supermarket somewhat aghast as the bill grew for drinks and food.

I need not have worried; the party was not only very
successful in that most people seemed to have a good time
but one of our guests - not even knowing how I had changed
my work - started discussing life assurance as a result of
which I sold a policy to cover the costs of the party.   Yet
again, money materialised from a most unexpected source.

* * * * * * *

At a conference on new forms of organisation in
business at Findhorn in 1987 I found myself busily buying
tapes of the various speakers' presentations.   What had
started as an attempt to buy one or two ended up with me
buying almost the whole collection.   However, not only did
I then have a collection of tapes to share with people but was
able to better consult them when writing an article on the
conference, the fee for which more than covered the cost of
the tapes I had bought.

* * * * * * *

Whilst on a visit to some friends in Scotland at Easter in
1989 Alan expressed a wish to hear a tape of music for
meditation which was sitting on the parcel shelf of the car.
I left the tape for him when we drove South again.   Three
weeks later my friendly astrologer in Keswick freely offered
to give me a tape of meditation music which I had particularly enjoyed during our consultation.

* * * * * * *

Some friends had dropped a note through our door
during a house to house collection for Amnesty International
inviting us to contribute when we returned.   A few days
later, when it felt appropriate, I walked down the road to put
a small donation through their door.   On the way back I
bumped into a friend with whom I used to play tennis and
who I had not seen for months.

We agreed to play the following day and my friend,
being an American, was able to guide me to a much cheaper
source of tickets for my forthcoming trip to the USA than I
had previously discovered.   The special deal I found also
included the hire of a car at a very reasonable rate with a
total saving of well over £100 on previous estimates.

* * * * * * *

On the spur of the moment one day I offered to take

my friend Rob out for lunch; nothing extravagant but a chance for me to repay some of his kindness to me.

On the way back to the office, sheltering in a large department store from a sudden shower, I found myself greeted by an old colleague who I had not seen for over a year. We arranged lunch, renewed our friendship and, some months later, I found myself processing her pension policy which more than paid for Rob's lunch.

* * * * * * *

You get the idea. The money we put out comes back to us; the love we put out comes back to us. The anger we put out comes back to us. The choice is ours.

Money, it seems, is like a signpost to our emotional battleground. When we understand how we treat money we have a clue as to how we treat other issues in our life. Are we hanging onto money - paying it at the last minute? What do we do with our emotions do we hang onto those as well? Maybe we will never have time enough to express them. Or do we pay our bills as we receive them, letting our love flow with our money.

The Barefoot Accountant

A few days ago I visited the house of a friend - barefoot as I had been all day. I had forgotten, however, that this drive had pebble dash gravel and I picked my way slowly and painfully over the twenty metres from the road to the front door. There has to be a better way than this, I thought.

By the time I was ready to leave I knew what to do. Just march straight over the pebbles, not pausing and certainly not waiting long enough to bathe in the pain they offered. I began to understand how people walk across burning coals although I don't think I could quite manage that - yet! If we linger over paying our fiscal and emotional dues we are going to find it as painful as walking slowly down that gravel drive.

The choice, as ever, is ours.

CHAPTER 22

HOW MANY MIRACLES?

Last autumn I sent out what I thought was the completed manuscript of this book to an agent who took two months to refuse it and then to a publisher in California who took three months to reach the same conclusion.

Meanwhile the miracles keep on happening and there has been such a stream in the month of March 1990 that it seemed appropriate to string them together in what - perhaps only temporarily - is the final chapter. Is there ever a final chapter?

This story begins back in 1989 when I first heard the album "Hearts and Bones" by Paul Simon. A number of the songs appealed to me greatly but there was something in particular about some of the lines in the title track that affected me most and for reasons that I could not clearly understand. "One and one half wandering Jews" was a particularly elliptical line - here I was, Jewish and apparently happily married to someone who was Jewish; why did I feel haunted by the line?

It went on "Free to wander wherever they choose" ah, now there was something that appealed to the Geminian restlessness that I share with my father. Still only a vague calling.

It was two lines further that the rub came. With diction so poor that I couldn't hear the words properly but had to check the reference on a map Paul Simon had sung of the "Sangre de Christo, Blood of Christ mountains in New Mexico." Over and over I listened to that song as the years went by and the marginal success of "Hearts and Bones" was subsumed by the thundering applause which greeted Paul Simon's next album, "Graceland."

For some reason of which I was not consciously aware the phrase remained with me, lodged in the back of my mind for use at a future date and for a future reason. In 1983, devoted to climbing the executive ladder in industrial Birmingham, England, New Mexico might as well have been on the moon.

The fascination with New Mexico - which broadened to

cover the general area of the other Southwestern States, Colorado, Arizona and Utah - surfaced again in September 1987 when I read "Dancing in the Light" by Shirley Maclaine. In the second half of the book - which I read at one three hour stretch at my desk across a very protracted lunch hour in Walsall - she described her work with the acupuncturist Chris Griscom at the Light Institute in Galisteo, New Mexico. Whilst I couldn't abide the idea of having needles stuck into me the results fascinated me.

My interest in the concept of re-incarnation had been awakening over the previous year and here, in glorious technicolour, Shirley Maclaine had been experiencing her past lives. Even more important, for me, was the revelation to her of her Higher Self, an androgynous figure in a blue cloak who was the real essence of that entity known as Shirley Maclaine.

This was the place where she went for true guidance - within herself - not to some external authority. And the guidance was always right, it was just a question of following it, of making the choice to listen. Her subsequent books, "All in the Playing" and "Going Within" continued her story along the same lines. Could I make the same journey? At that stage I was not prepared to recognise that we each have our own individual journey to make.

A month after reading the book I was at a conference at Findhorn and met Lesley from Salt Lake City who casually told me that her own teacher in Utah did past life work without resorting to needles - perhaps that might be a more suitable option for me?

Hm, there was still something about New Mexico which seemed to be calling. A year later Lesley sent me a personal account of a session she had had exploring her past lives and of the conference where we had met; it was a fascinating story in which I read of my own part in the process - still it was New Mexico that interested me and, someone, somewhere, passed on the information that they had stopped using needles at the Light Institute. I looked at the brochure I had in my drawer and told myself I would get there someday.

At this stage I was coping with the aftermath of marital separation, particularly the pain of not seeing much of my children, and was about to become self-employed. New Mexico seemed as far away as ever.

What I did notice, however, was that people kept popping up in my life with a connection to the Southwestern

states.   The daughter of a good friend living in Gibraltar at
the time got a college place in Montezuma, NM;   I got to
know the Emissary Foundation, one of whose worldwide
intentional spiritual communities is in Boulder, Colorado.
There would be "chance" meetings with people who had
connections to that part of the world and I read "Star Signs"
by Linda Goodman which also talked about those Sangre de
Christo mountains.   Someone else said they felt - when I was
describing these events - that I had certainly had a very happy
lifetime somewhere in that area probably as an Indian.   Then
I found an exhibition in Walsall (of all places) of American
Indian life and it felt like it would have been a Navajo Indian.
But how could I know?   How could I be certain of anything
anymore?

In the Autumn of 1989 with the prospect of a financial
settlement being reached on my jointly owned house it
looked as though there would be some money available to go
to New Mexico.   The whole project including flight, car hire
and fees was probably going to cost around £1500.   It was
an idea which had been with me for two full years.   Had I
changed in that time?   The first tranche of money for the
trip was readily obtained and came about as a result of my
starting to tithe.

I had made a trip to the Eastern part of the USA in
August of 1989 in order to give a workshop called "Your
Money or your Life."   The trip had cost very little apart
from the air fare due to the wonderful and spontaneous
hospitality we had enjoyed.   In a bookstore on 5th Avenue
in New York I had come across a book by Catherine Ponder
called "Open Your Mind to Prosperity" which, amongst
other things, had dealt with the idea of tithing - donating one
tenth part of all money you receive to people or ideas which
give you spiritual inspiration.

The idea was rooted in Biblical times and although I had
come across it in the modern world occasionally I had not
felt ready to actually take part in the practice myself.   The
odd gift here and there - or even my annual charity payment
described earlier - was one thing but 10% of everything well,
I knew the theory that what goes out must come back but
10% of everything sounded a bit steep.   However, on my
return from the States I felt ready to do this and where
better to begin, I thought, than with Helen, who had coun-
selled me in 1986/87 and for who knows how many other
lifetimes?   With a large family and what I recalled as a
chronic lack of money although abundant wisdom and
humour she would surely be glad of the cash.

117

The other thing I love about Helen is her honesty and after I had made my little speech and handed over the cheque she told me that things had improved considerably over the past few months (I had not seen her for some time) and she really did not need the money. The discussion went on for a little while and we became blocked as she was, I think, loathe to reject the gift although not really needing it. Eventually the conversation moved on and I told her that I was now definitely planning to go to the Light Institute in March 1990 to uncover my past lives. It was as though a spring had been released and the money came flying back to me.

"This is my present to you," she said, "towards the trip!"

I wavered for a minute wondering what rules of tithing I would be breaking by giving the money to myself but realised that I had fully released the money from my consciousness to Helen and could accept her gift.

Although I didn't realise it at the time, the gift was almost exactly the amount I needed to send to the Light Institute as a deposit for the past life sessions.

I called Richard at the Light Institute to tell him I wanted to come and he said he would get in touch when he could schedule time. I was nervous.

For some unaccountable reason I became more nervous and then I became nervous about the fact that I was nervous, recalling other trips which I had planned and about which I had felt surges of excitement. If this was a trip of a lifetime (or several lifetimes) then why was I not feeling the same way now?

Dianne turned up to stay with us for a night in December on *her* trip of a lifetime from the States to Europe. The post dinner conversation turned to my proposed trip and I expressed my doubts; she had heard nothing bad about the Light Institute although she thought the fees ($1000 per week) were high - I caught a glimmer of the idea that I was finding someone to mirror my own feelings; it did seem a lot yet in commercial terms this was not excessive and I would be the first to commend establishing self esteem by charging what you believe you are worth - the trick is catching yourself before overstepping that line to greediness.

The conversation closed with my feeling that it was probably OK and the following morning a letter arrived from Richard saying that he could now schedule time and would I get in touch to finalise arrangements. It was a letter which I felt was both sincere and honest - surely it would be OK to go?

How Many Miracles?

Two days later my friend Peter (who lives in Zurich) turns up in Birmingham to the opening of our bookshop (another story entirely) and on learning that I am planning to go to NM promises to put me in touch with a management centre that is committed to helping business executives discover the more intuitive part of themselves - a subject dear to my heart - and the sort of establishment which I had ideas of helping create in Birmingham. One day?

That Peter, who I had not seen for more than a year, should accept my throwaway invitation to come to the opening of the bookshop during the middle of a three week spell in London and provide me with a contact in Santa Fe - the exact town for which I was headed - seemed further validation of my planned trip - except a little part of me wondered why I was looking for validation anyway.

The new decade started and I thumbed through my Earthstewards Network listing to find if there was anyone with whom I could stay in Santa Fe - on a paying basis if necessary - rather than the impersonal surroundings of a bed and breakfast. There was one name out of a list of four hundred.

I telephoned, found a friendly answering machine and left a message to say that I would be writing.

I set to work arranging the flight and after weighing up the various options of flying to Alberquerqe - which was nearer but to which I could not get a direct flight - or to Denver to which I could get a direct flight but which meant a three hundred mile drive I opted for Denver with the prospect of actually driving through the Sangre de Christo mountains whose ethereal presence in my consciousness would soon be seen in physical form.

I booked the flight after many telephone calls and felt a sense more of inevitability rather than excitement although I tried to overcome this by telling people about my trip with some enthusiasm. Two people, however, who I had thought would be very interested and who were familiar with the idea of past lives were actually rather surprised and wondered why I was going.

Then I found myself being more evasive about the whole trip. I would tell people I was going to New Mexico but only respond to their questions about purpose with some vague mutterings about always having wanted to go there or needing to get away for a week - both of which were true but both of which avoided the issue.

I now had the name of a contact with whom to stay on my first night in Denver and had received a positive response

119

to my request for accommodation but had still not heard from my contact in Santa Fe for accommodation there.

I telephoned Richard at the Light Institute to confirm the sessions and to ask him to send me a list of local Bed and Breakfasts.   I don't know what it was but he sounded slightly less warm than when I had spoken to him four months previously.   Perhaps I had chosen a morning when his new baby had kept him awake and his less cordial tone had provided me with an excuse to doubt.

It was late February and I was feeling distinctly uneasy.

I visited my friend Helena who was living in a community near Wolverhampton and finally met the founder of the community, Manny Patel, whom I had managed to avoid in eight months of visiting Helena and about whom I had all sorts of preconceptions as some great authority figure - probably in a black coat and Rabbinical beard which seems to be the scenario from which much of my desire to rebel originates.

As soon as Manny walked in the room I felt a glow of connection with him, a warm lovable man in his late thirties, I suppose, whose Hindu upbringing and practices seemed to hold as much affection for him as Judaism did to me.

Where I wanted to rebel, however, he just seemed to accept things and to flow with it; we spent two hours talking about religion and spirituality; crucially, how all religions lead to the same thing, something I have known for years but which never seemed to go down well in the traditional Jewish circles in which I had mixed.   If I could only learn that the truth is no less the truth just because someone else chooses not to see it as such.   Or maybe there is no such thing as absolute truth.

A sister centre to the one in Wolverhampton had been set up in Colorado Springs. Manny told me that a number of the people there were Jewish, perhaps I could spend some time with them on my trip; we would be sure to have much in common. He was certainly very doubtful about my doing past life work, thought it would raise more questions for me and that at the moment I needed answers, not questions. It was a lovely conversation and I left feeling even more unsure about what to do.

I had an air ticket to Denver and a reservation (deposit paid) at the Light Institute, somewhere to stay for a night in Denver, people I could visit in Colorado Springs or Boulder, Colorado and the whole of the Sangre de Christo mountains to explore.

How Many Miracles?

I was due to see Helen the following day for the first time in months and I told her that I had the trip planned for two weeks hence. She enthused about the idea of past life work and told me that she was going to do some herself in Puerto Rico at the end of March. She had also been reading past lives for people recently.

So here I was again; not for the first time in my life I had set up two people who I totally respected and who had totally different viewpoints about what to do. The words of Rabbi Hillel came back to me "If I am not for myself then who is for me; and if not now, when?" Dammit! Was *I* actually going to have to decide for myself whether I should go to these sessions - would no-one do it for me?

To compound matters I had recently had a letter from Dianne saying how, despite the doubts I had raised with her during her visit in December, my subsequent (enthusiastic) letter gave her a good feeling about my forthcoming trip.

I also knew that my partner, Jane, never normally restrictive in what I do was distinctly uneasy about the trip and had been since it was first mooted. Whether it was the past life analysis, the thought of me on my own on the 'plane or a combination of them both I don't know but I was recognising in her a concern which I knew was not manipulative and which seemed to come from a higher source - devout agnostic as she is!

One of the things which had puzzled me was the lack of funds to actually pay for the trip. Working on the assumption that money is there if you need it this did not seem a very helpful indication.

The process of extricating some money from my share of the house had become protracted and, while business had kept at a reasonable level through the winter, the amount of time I had put into getting the bookshop open and the collapse of a couple of hoped-for deals had all contributed to a financial situation which was not as rosy as it might have been. Even the discovery that, despite clear instructions to the contrary, five months life insurance premiums on a policy I was about to terminate had not been collected still left me several hundred pounds short.

I spoke to my travel agent to ask what proportion of the fare, if any, I might reclaim should I cancel the trip. They seemed quite clear that as the flight departure was only two weeks away I would lose all my money - £478.

On the evening of Friday 23rd. February I telephoned the Pecos River Learning Centre in Santa Fe to see whether

121

I might spend a little of my limited free time in New Mexico with them learning how they loosen up burned out executives. The telephone connection was quick and clear across six thousand miles and the coil began to unwind.

The connection to Pecos River Learning Centre had been so easy that I decided to jettison the trip to the Light Institute but as I still had a ticket for Denver and a rented car for a week I would take the flight, visit the Centre and be open to whatever else happened - a Springtime adventure. And anyway, as I'd paid for the ticket I might as well use it, never mind that by making the trip I would spend more than if I stayed at home. Whatever had happened to the Investment Appraisal techniques I had learned as an ambitious trainee accountant? Rule one: past costs are *always* ignored.

At that stage I believed that the idea of going to the Light Institute had been a peg on which to hang the idea of getting myself to a part of the USA to which I felt called. I clearly didn't respect myself enough to just say that that was what I needed to do. Jane would probably not have objected even if I had expressed this wish but the experience of being in a marriage where this sort of issue had loomed large was taking time to be transformed.

I walked around on the Saturday feeling pleased that I had exercised the right to cancel, to let go of something, to not feel bound by an idea. OK, so I would probably lose the deposit I had paid to the Light Institute but I had given that money away once anyway! The money I saved in fees would come in useful some other way.

There was of course, a little part of me that was asking how I was going to get my guidance now that I had decided not to keep that appointment with my Higher Self but, just for that Saturday that voice was ignored.

On the Sunday morning (New Moon at 8.54 a.m. GMT) I woke up with a sinking feeling and I knew that the process had not yet finished. There was a further release to come. In my mind's eye I could see aeroplanes crashing and having to come back in another lifetime if I played truant from this one in order to learn some incomplete lessons. It would be the first time in eighteen months that Jane and I would be out of ready contact with each other and she seemed particularly vulnerable at that time. Not to say tired after working flat out in a new life in the bookshop for the last three months with only minimal time off over Christmas and a taxing rehearsal schedule for a forthcoming amateur play.

With that vision of crashing aeroplanes I had to ask myself whether it was more important to let go of the £478 I had paid for flight, car hire and medical insurance or, as I then believed, fall out of the sky from thirty thousand feet?

For one brought up to know the value of money from an early age, through the accumulated responsibilities of Treasurer of the Scout Social Club, Treasurer of the Jewish Students Society and Financial Director of a large engineering company this was not an easy matter. In fact the whole thing seemed a complete mess. But, faced with the option of making that release or freefall skydiving without a parachute the act of release won the day.

I told Jane who was watching my contorted, tear-laden face with her customary steadfastness that I felt my place was with her at this time and that I wasn't going to New Mexico.

Within an hour a large number of bits of the jigsaw of my life fell into place one after the other. The five day holiday which Jane and I had planned for May but which she badly needed now and which had been proving very difficult to arrange could be taken in the week I had booked for New Mexico; people to look after Kate, Jane's daughter, and Hoopers, our bookshop, were immediately available with a couple of telephone calls and in one of those calls a conversation took place which promised, after eighteen months blockage, to start the resolution of the aftermath of Jane's own marriage.

On the Monday I toyed with the idea of calling the travel agents to formally cancel my flight but thought there really was no point in doing so as there was no money to come back. Instead I went into our local travel agent (as opposed to the one with whom I had been dealing in the centre of Birmingham) to make a last minute booking for Jane and I to go to Paris by rail and hovercraft (due heed to economy at this stage!). The agent tried solidly for five minutes to contact the holiday company but the 'phone was busy and I realised that I should move on somewhere else.

From our bookshop a few doors away I decided to telephone to cancel my flight to Denver and enquired on the offchance whether I would get any money back. They did not know. They would call be back. Two hours later I was in town and called into the travel agents. Any chance of a refund?

With no great concern they told me that I would get everything back except my £50 deposit and £28 medical insurance. But it might be some time before the £400 came through as they couldn't pay out until they had been reimbursed by the airline. Would that be OK, they asked?

Since they were so downbeat I, who had not expected anything, restrained myself from letting out a shout of delight and said, as nonchalantly as I could manage, that it would be fine, I didn't mind waiting. Within five minutes I had booked with them for five days in Paris - the last two places on the train - and at a substantially lower price than we had planned to spend in May.

I wondered whether I would have to hassle over the coming months in order to get the refund but, to my surprise, when my next credit card statement was delivered a couple of weeks later the refund had already been credited.

"How many miracles," I had asked my friend Arabella to whom I related this story, "do I need before I truly accept the constancy of the Divine Presence?"

Unhesitatingly the answer came back "As many as it takes."

How Many Miracles?

I guess that's true for everyone and although I had planned to write of some of the other wonders that have occurred this strange Spring I think further individual case studies would be unnecessary.

How strange (or was it?) that I should have spoken to someone on the Friday who had given me completely the wrong idea either out of ignorance or carelessness but also how certain that I had examined my life much more deeply in the light of that misinformation.

Yet again money had been a medium through which to view the mess into which I had got my life at that time. The frequently recurring theme had been the difficulty experienced in letting go of something. In this case it had been £478 together with an idea which I had formulated two years previously that I must go to the Light Institute. Having fallen for a number of "get rich quick" schemes over the years - see previous chapters - I had now done the same thing but on a different level.

I had looked at the Light Institute as a "spiritual get rich quick scheme" - $1000 for instant enlightenment and visual access to your Higher Self - rather than simply another stage on the Journey. I started to look around me and realise there were a large number of pretty wonderful people who had never even heard of the Light Institute - let alone planned to take sessions there!

That is not to denigrate in any way the work that goes on in Galisteo, New Mexico. I believe their work to be extremely valuable and have found much wisdom in Chris Griscom's books. However, what was important for me was to recognise that we each make our own spiritual journey and the inner certainty I feel when it is right to do something is simply the way in which my own Higher Self seems to manifest.

By way of analogy, the "Inner Voice" of Eileen Caddy, co-founder of Findhorn, is well chronicled but husband Peter admitted that he had never once heard such a voice and simply acted on what he called an "Inner prompting." It is that notion which is closer to what I feel.

Doing what you *feel* is right, not what some little "ought" from someone else tells you, that is the secret, and it works on a day to day level.

To take a recent example; last week I finished watching a rugby match on the television and was unsure whether to cook something for dinner (the logical thing as it was mid-afternoon) or do the ironing which had to be done but could

125

wait until the following day. I felt like doing the ironing and went ahead. Half an hour later some friends telephoned with an impromptu invitation to join them for a celebratory dinner that evening. I was delighted to accept and glad that I had followed my feelings to do the ironing and was not faced with a half prepared meal which was not required!

Which brings me to a clearer understanding of what this spiritual search is about. It's about concentrating on getting the details right in the here and now, about seeing what is in front of you - I began to realise this when I fell over the cat a few weeks ago! My mind had been in distant parts and I had missed what was under my nose.

Pay attention to what is in your daily life and do it with love. The answers to life are to be found in the streets of Birmingham as much as in the mountains of New Mexico. It took a lot to admit this as it was the sort of thing my ex-wife used to say and I found a certain amount of difficulty in conceding that *anything* she said might hold water! Maybe we will yet be friends again.

The story is the same in whatever culture. I understand that the Venerable Bede who lived in North East England many centuries ago never travelled more than twelve miles from his house and yet his teachings are rich in wisdom. The ancient teachings of Lao Tzu contained in chapter forty-seven of the Tao Te Ching put it succinctly:

"Without going outside you may know the whole world. Without looking through the window you may see the ways of Heaven. The farther you go, the less you know.

Thus the sage knows without travelling; He sees without looking; He works without doing."

At the point at which I decided not to make the trip, on the Sunday morning, I was consciously turning over the ways in which I could view my decision. On the one hand I could say that I had "lost" £500 but, on the other hand, I could claim to have learned some very valuable lessons without having had to spend the additional £1000 had I got on the 'plane - assuming it didn't crash! It all depends on the way you look at things.

The two incidents with the money, both my tithe to Helen being re-presented and the loosening up of Jane's affairs which would impinge on my own situation not to mention the refund on the tickets which came from nowhere

126

clarified a Bible story I had re-read some months previously.

It was the story of Abraham who was willing to sacrifice his son, Isaac, because God had so commanded him. It was a story which has also been told in song by Leonard Cohen and the notion had haunted me as much in the song as the original story had when I was a child. How could one ever justify the sacrifice of a child?

But, of course, Isaac does not die, and I believe the crucial point of the story is about our *willingness* to sacrifice to what is the highest good. The trick, of course, is knowing what is the highest good and that knowledge is only available when we are contacting the deepest part of us. What *feels* best, is not always the same as what we *think* is best but so many of us have been brought up never to let our hearts (where we feel) rule our heads (where we think).

Rational thought is a wonderful gift but there has been a tendency to over use it of late.

The specific example in the Bible is a graphic one in order to make the point and whether it actually happened that way on Mount Moriah or not is almost irrelevant for the myth is what is important - the feeling behind the story, the archetype rather than the specific incident.

Once I had been willing to sacrifice my £478 the much needed break for Jane had arranged itself, we had the welcome news that her post matrimonial affairs were starting to unravel and I recovered £400 I had never expected to see again.

My money, or energy, had come back only after I had been prepared to release it totally. And as it is with money so it is with people; money as the indicator to relationships. Once we release someone from any obligation we may pretend they have to us then they will return of their own free will.

It is one of those tantalising and unanswerable questions to conjecture what would have happened had I made the trip. I checked the newspapers on the dates when I should have flown but nothing crashed.

Whether I eventually make a trip to New Mexico I don't know at this stage and although I had re-assessed the purpose of the trip from being one of exploring my past lives to one of learning how to get in touch with myself a certain interest remained in my past lives.

This came to light when I was receiving a healing from my friend Rob - he was actually using me as a guinea pig for the class he was running on how to heal through projecting

127

colours from the mind of the healer onto the afflicted areas
of the body. I mentioned that for no apparent reason I had
an image of a castle in my mind and he said, very casually,
that I had slipped back into a past life. In a flash I knew
that there was nothing intrinsically wrong for me in exploring
past lives but that I should continue to work with the fact
that everything you need in your life is very close to you if
only you look.

I remembered that my erstwhile counsellor and benefac-
tress, Helen, had said she was reading past lives for people
and two weeks later I was sitting in the chair in her room
where I had first sat three years previously.

With no great fuss she proceeded to read the past lives
which she saw in my aura. Again, it was the matter-of-
factness which was so striking; no needles, no need for a nine
hour flight and great expenditure, just a modest fee. As I
closed my eyes and listened to her I began to see additional
images to the ones she was describing which helped me
understand much of what is happening in my life at the
present time.

But that, as they say, is another story.

We have to believe in ourselves and when we connect
with whoever or whatever we perceive God to be then our
actions will have a certain rightness about them that otherwise is missing.

It is no longer relevant to me to engage in a debate
about whether God is a remote figure with a white beard in
the sky or an androgynous figure in a blue cowl arising in the
mind's eye. As I move from minute to minute there is
always the choice to flow with the Life Force and let it flow
through me or to bang my head on one more brick wall
which, for some unaccountable reason, I still seem to do at
times!

But then, learning to do it right is why I'm here. Gosh,
did I finally find an answer to what I thought was an
unanswerable question, endlessly debated from chalky
schoolrooms through coffee-filled nights at university to
executive dining rooms.

I believe I did, there *is* no goal, only process. Making
the one hundred and forty seven break on the snooker table,
selling a large insurance policy or even getting this book
published are meaningless unless I have actually enjoyed
doing it.

We have all suffered enough.